A LONG, DANGEROUS COASTLINE

Shipwreck Tales from Alaska to California

ANTHONY DALTON

VICTORIA · VANCOUVER · CALGARY

Heritage House Publishing Company Ltd.
www.heritagehouse.ca

Library and Archives Canada Cataloguing in Publication
Dalton, Anthony, 1940–
    A long, dangerous coastline: shipwreck tales from Alaska to California / Anthony Dalton.

Includes bibliographical references and index.
ISBN 978-1-926613-73-4

    1. Shipwrecks—Northwest Coast of North America—History—Anecdotes. 2. Passenger ships—Northwest Coast of North America—History—Anecdotes. 3. Northwest Coast of North America—History—Anecdotes. I. Title.

F851.D34 2010   979.5   C2010-904733-8

Series editor: Lesley Reynolds.
Proofreader: Karla Decker.
Cover design: Chyla Cardinal. Interior design: Frances Hunter.
Cover photo: USS *Nicholas* and USS *S.P. Lee*, wrecked at Honda Point, September 1923. US Naval Historical Center #NH84820.

 Mixed Sources
Cert no. SW-COC-001271
© 1996 FSC
FSC   The interior of this book was produced using 100% post-consumer recycled paper, processed chlorine free and printed with vegetable-based inks.

Heritage House acknowledges the financial support for its publishing program from the Government of Canada through the Canada Book Fund (CBF), Canada Council for the Arts and the province of British Columbia through the British Columbia Arts Council and the Book Publishing Tax Credit.

 Canada Council **Conseil des Arts**
for the Arts **du Canada**   BRITISH COLUMBIA
ARTS COUNCIL
Supported by the Province of British Columbia

13 12 11 10   1 2 3 4 5
Printed in Canada

For all those who work to improve safety at sea

Contents

Prologue

THE NORTH WIND SHRIEKED ACROSS *the decks from one end to the other and buffeted the stricken ship. She still had engine power, and black smoke poured from her funnel to show there was life in her yet. The wind, however, whipped the smoke away horizontally to the south before it could climb into the sky and dissipate naturally. The storm was building in intensity. The sea was rough; white caps topped waves that were getting bigger and bolder with the passing minutes. The ship creaked and groaned, uncomfortable where she sat stranded but upright on a broad, flat ledge of rock.*

The Canadian Pacific steamship Princess Sophia *had been aground on Vanderbilt Reef in the Lynn Canal for over 14 hours. Many of her passengers braved the dreadful late-afternoon fall* weather to watch a few smaller rescue vessels milling about not far away. The sea was too rough to launch the Princess' lifeboats to take the passengers and crew clear of the reef, but the rescue boats waited anyway, giving those aboard the stranded ship assurance that they would get off safely.

On the bridge, Captain Locke and other officers smoked their cigarettes and pipes. They listened to the screaming wind and watched the driving snow and the building seas. They displayed an aura of confidence to the passengers, but that was just a bold nautical front. Deep inside, each man had his own doubts, his own demons. Each officer was wondering how this shipwreck would play out.

Despite the increasing waves and the gale howling around his ship, Captain Locke expressed his satisfaction that the Princess and all aboard her were in no immediate danger. But he was concerned for the safety of the rescue ships. Taking a megaphone, he stepped out into the open and bellowed across the water to one of them, "We are perfectly safe; you better go into harbour until morning."

They left but were soon replaced by larger ships, which circled the reef for a couple of hours. There was nothing more they could do until the storm and the waves died down. Eventually, they too retreated out of the wind to safe anchorages not far away. At 8:00 p.m., a steam pipe fractured and all the lights went out on the Princess. A few lanterns soon showed, but without the bright lights from saloons and cabins, the ship suddenly appeared more fragile.

Prologue

Snow and sleet and winds gusting to 100 miles per hour ravaged the ship. Another 24 hours of uncertainty passed for passengers and crew. There was still no possibility of taking anyone off. The storm increased in ferocity, and the driving snow created whiteout conditions.

In the late afternoon of the second day on the reef, as the gale-force north wind continued to pound against the aft quarter of the Princess, *slowly her stern and propeller lifted off the rock, and she began to move.*

Introduction

THE SEA IS INCAPABLE OF showing emotion, yet it can be angry. It is incapable of showing respect for ships or for the men who sail in them, but it demands respect anyway. The ever-moving sea is a law and an entity unto itself. It washes and erodes rocks and cliffs with restless persistence. In concert with the wind, it changes coastlines at will. The fragile ships and the men that sail in them on her waters are insignificant intruders in an alien and often dangerous domain.

Ships have been sailing the west coast of the North American continent since at least the 16th century, when Spanish explorers probed north of the equator. They were followed by a steady stream of British ships. These voyagers were all there in the spirit of exploration, seeking to discover and claim new lands for their monarchs and to trade with locals wherever they might be found.

By the late 18th century, trading forts had been established from the Columbia River to Vancouver Island and the mainland of what is now British Columbia. Although separated from the rest of the nation by a wild and often lawless land, California had been annexed into the United States. The sea lanes along the coasts of California, Oregon, Washington, British Columbia and parts of Alaska began to be travelled by more and more ships.

In the 19th and 20th centuries, accidents became more frequent as marine traffic increased dramatically. Where once ships occasionally were lost off the coast during storms, shipwrecks began to happen more often on the foggy shores. In addition, collisions at sea between ships travelling in opposite directions added to the losses of ships, passengers and crews.

The 14 short stories in this book are about shipwrecks along the west coast of North America between California and Alaska. Studying the events that led to the accidents shows that, in most cases, human error cost the lives of the people lost in the disasters. Human error wrecked many of the ships, and human error was responsible for the loss of the cargoes on board. Sadly, human error continues to be a major cause of accidents at sea. The advancement of technology, it seems, is no guarantee of safety.

1

On Anacapa's Foggy Shores

THE NEW YORK–BASED SHIPBUILDING company of Westervelt & MacKay proudly launched their latest creation in late October 1850. As the wooden-hulled sidewheel steamer slid down the ways for the first time, her entry into the east-coast waters was heralded with cheers of appreciation.

Winfield Scott was an elegant ship for her time. She sported a sharply pointed bow with an elongated bowsprit. In addition, she carried three masts: one forward of her funnel and two abaft. Her sail plan included three foresails, or jibs, square-rigged canvas on the foremast with a gaff abaft, and gaff-rigged sails on the main and mizzen-masts. With all sails set and the steam engine working hard, she was fast and she was strong. Surprisingly for a sidewheel steamer, she appears to have been quite stable and seaworthy on heavy ocean swells, unlike many of her counterparts.

Winfield Scott was registered at 1,292 tons. Like most sidewheel steamers, she was long and lean, apart from the bulky paddlewheels on each side. She was 225 feet in length and had a beam of 34.7 feet. Despite her relatively slim hull, she held accommodations for 165 people in cabins, with room for a further 150 passengers in steerage class.

For the first two years of her service, *Winfield Scott* (named after the famed US Army general who served his country on active duty for over 50 years—longer than any other American) carried passengers between New York City and New Orleans for Davis, Brooks & Company. In 1852, she was sold to the New York & San Francisco Steamship Company for service on the west coast. Following a six-month voyage around the southern tip of South America, she arrived in San Francisco on April 18, 1852. Her new route was to be San Francisco to Panama and return, first for the Independent Line until the end of 1852, then for the New York & San Francisco Steamship Company from February to April 1853. In July 1853, she was purchased by the Pacific Mail Steamship Company.

In the middle of the 19th century and the following decades leading up to the completion of the Panama Canal, people migrating to the newly annexed state of California from the eastern seaboard had the choice of three routes. The first and most direct route was a difficult, expensive and often dangerous overland journey that took settlers through large tracts of hostile territory. The second was the long haul by sea down the Atlantic through the notoriously turbulent Drake Passage or Straits of Magellan at the southern tip of the Americas and up the west coast of South and Central America to Los Angeles or San Francisco. The third and final route was by sea to the Isthmus of Panama, then a jungle trek of over 50 miles from the Caribbean Sea to the Pacific Ocean. From there, with few ships available, passengers might have to wait for long periods of time, often many weeks, for a berth on a northbound ship. *Winfield Scott*'s west-coast positioning was intended to help alleviate this problem. One year after the sidewheeler arrived on the west coast, her owners changed their name to the Pacific Mail Steamship Company.

Winfield Scott soon became a popular ship, known to run the route comfortably and safely. She carried immigrants north and gold seekers south. It was a profitable arrangement for the company and good for the travellers.

On December 1, 1853, the sidewheel steamer's whistle announced her departure as she slipped her moorings in the port of San Francisco. As usual, she was outward bound for a reasonably fast run down the coast to Panama. On board, the crew went about their work while a full complement of passengers settled down for the night. In the holds, the ship carried a reported $2 million in gold bullion.

Captain Simon Blunt guided his ship out through the

Golden Gate to the open sea and turned south. Problems with a leaking boiler slowed the ship for a while in the afternoon. To make up the lost time once it had been repaired, Blunt chose to run at full speed though the Santa Barbara Channel. The weather was good, and having been instrumental in the marine survey of the Santa Barbara Channel a few years earlier, he knew the area between the mainland and the Channel Islands intimately. But weather conditions at sea can change quickly, and they did so late that night.

Cleaving her way through the rolling seas at her best speed, the ship entered a thick fog bank. Captain Blunt slowed his charge down to about 10 knots and maintained his course. Unfortunately, without the captain's knowledge, the current had set *Winfield Scott* some distance west of the planned track. Hidden in the darkness and fog, the over-900-foot heights of West Anacapa Island passed unseen. The sheer cliffs of the much lower Middle Anacapa Island followed. The sea was rough, and although the sounds did not reach the ship, breaking waves pounded the rocks at the base of the cliffs.

Sometime after 11:00 p.m. on that first night of the voyage, *Winfield Scott*, running blind by dead reckoning and drifting off course, aided by a current, smashed her bow through the breakers and onto the southeastern end of Middle Anacapa Island. A passenger told of the impact and of hearing the "crashing of timbers."

Captain Blunt tried to back her off, but the action of

The sidewheel steamer *Winfield Scott* was wrecked on Middle Anacapa Island in the Santa Barbara Channel in early December 1853. CHANNEL ISLANDS NATIONAL MARINE SANCTUARY

the waves caused the ship to swing sideways. The stern also struck the rocks with enough force to rip off the rudder. Knowing that *Winfield Scott* was holed and taking on water fast and there was no possibility of steering her to safety, Blunt gave the order for all to abandon ship. Fortunately for the passengers and crew, they were able to clamber off the stricken ship and onto solid ground without getting too wet. Within two hours, everyone was landed safely on a confined piece of reasonably level, spray-lashed rock measuring roughly 50 by 25 yards. At daybreak, better able to assess the situation, Captain Blunt shepherded his charges to a safer position on the island. At that time, *Winfield Scott* was still partly afloat.

The SS *California* was steaming north from Panama to San Francisco while *Winfield Scott* was battering herself to death on the rocks of Middle Anacapa Island. She passed in daylight after the night's fog had cleared. One of the survivors from the wrecked ship, presumably a crew member, fired a gun, and an observant person on *California* saw the puff of smoke and reported it to the captain. *California* steamed in close but kept a safe distance from the wreck and the shore. The crew launched boats, and soon all the women and children had been taken off their exposed position on the island and were safely aboard the northbound vessel. The gold bullion was also rescued at that time. One week later, having delivered its passengers and the gold back to San Francisco, *California* returned for the remaining passengers—all men. The crew, however, stayed on the island, working hard to take off the mails and as much of the freight and passengers' baggage as possible before their sidewheeler went down. They were later collected and also taken back to San Francisco.

A shipping disaster that could have resulted in a terrible tragedy became a successful rescue. No one died. The most valuable cargo and most of the passengers' personal effects were saved. The only loss was the ship, and that became the insurance underwriters' problem. Ecologically, in addition to the wreckage of the ship, the incident was disastrous for the island. Obeying the unwritten natural law about abandoning a sinking ship, untold numbers of rats fled *Winfield Scott* and took up residence on the island. Multiplying rapidly, they roamed Anacapa foraging for food, and there they discovered a liking for birds' eggs. Their predations had a devastating effect on the seabird populations.

There was no possibility of salvaging the ship. *Winfield Scott* had suffered too much damage in the breakers. She eventually settled in about 30 feet of water. For the next four decades, she stayed there undisturbed. In 1894, efforts were made to salvage as much useful material as possible. The iron machinery was hauled up, and a large number of copper bolts were recovered and recycled. After that, she was left in peace for another few decades. During the Second World War, however, with metals of all kinds desperately needed for the war effort, a new salvage operation brought up more iron and brass.

Winfield Scott's sister ship, *California*, continued in the coastal trade for various companies until 1875. Then her engines and paddles were removed, and she was converted to a sailing ship. Reduced to carrying coal and lumber, she was wrecked on the coast of Peru in late 1894. Neither ship lost any passengers or crew. Others would not be so fortunate.

2

Brother Jonathan: Lost on St. George's Reef

BROTHER JONATHAN WAS ANOTHER wooden-hulled sidewheel steamer with auxiliary sails built on the east coast of the US. She came from the shipyard of Perrine, Patterson & Stack, in Williamsburg, New York, in 1851. Registered at 1,360 tons, she was 220.9 feet in length and had a beam of 36 feet. She carried a single mast suited with square-rigged sails. She was designed and built for Edward Mills and had accommodation for 365 passengers. Planned for many years of service, *Brother Jonathan* slid down the ways at her builder's shipyard on November 2, 1850.

For her first two years, *Brother Jonathan* sailed between New York and Chagres, Panama. When she was sold to Cornelius Vanderbilt in 1852, he added a mizzen-mast and gaff sail for stability and increased her profile by adding a third deck, which more than doubled her passenger capacity to 750 persons. It would also have made her more susceptible to rolling in heavy seas or strong winds. Once she had been refurbished, she sailed around South America from New York to San Francisco. Vanderbilt's company then sailed her between San Francisco and San Juan del Sur, Nicaragua.

Sold again in 1856, this time to a Captain John T. Wright, she was renamed *Commodore* and sent north. In those days, more so than now, it was considered bad luck to change a ship's name, so the superstitious among her crew and passengers must have occasionally had doubts about the wisdom of doing so. Despite that possible drawback, her new route would be from San Francisco to Victoria and on to Puget Sound ports, just in time for the Fraser River gold rush. In a bid to make money as fast as possible, *Commodore* often sailed overloaded with passengers and cargo. In July 1858, that desire for profit almost caused her loss.

Commodore ran into a heavy storm while steaming north and almost went to the bottom. The crew began to toss everything movable over the side to keep her afloat. That meant cargo, passengers' baggage and crew possessions all had to go before the ship could be turned back to San Francisco. No doubt there were those who blamed the name change for the near disaster.

Captain Wright sold *Commodore* to the California

Steam Navigation Company in 1861. They put her through another overhaul, sensibly removing the third deck Vanderbilt had installed years before and replacing a number of rotten hull planks. They also sealed her bottom in copper plate to prevent teredo worms destroying the wood of her hull. The only item not replaced was her aging engine, which had started life long before in a different ship. Once she was ready for sea, her new owners changed her name back to *Brother Jonathan.*

The modernized ship now received a new master: Captain Samuel De Wolf, a 40-year-old lifelong mariner born in Nova Scotia. For a few years, *Brother Jonathan* continued on the San Francisco–Portland–Victoria–Puget Sound route. Most of the voyages were relatively uneventful, although there was a report that she had collided with a sailing ship near Portland, without suffering noticeable damage. But her time was running out.

Brother Jonathan left San Francisco in mid-morning on Friday, July 30, 1865. As usual, she was bound for Portland, then Victoria. Soon after getting out on the open ocean, the sidewheeler ran into a gale and heavy seas. *Brother Jonathan* had proved many times that she could handle big seas, even with those cumbersome-looking paddlewheels on each side of her hull. She had sailed from New York, down the Atlantic, around Tierra del Fuego and up the west coast of the Americas. Although she was never a really fast ship, *Brother Jonathan* had developed a reputation for being the fastest sidewheel steamer on the San Francisco–Portland–Victoria run. It was said she could make the voyage in 69 hours of steaming.

On the fateful voyage, *Brother Jonathan*'s passenger list of 124 included a mix of the rich and the not-so-rich, the important and the unknown. Her officers and crew added another 54 names. There were reports of a few last-minute additions to the passenger complement, but if so, the manifest did not register that fact. Among the well-known people on board were Brigadier General George Wright and his wife. They were bound for Portland, where the general was to take up his new position as commander of the Columbia District, based at Fort Vancouver on the Columbia River. Wright's aide-de-camp, Lieutenant E. Waite, and his wife were travelling as part of the general's party. Another officer en route to Fort Vancouver was Major F. Eddy. He was the army paymaster and carried some $200,000 of government money—probably in gold coins—to pay the soldiers garrisoned in Washington and Oregon. Also on board was another important man, Dr. Anson Henry. He was the newly appointed governor of Washington. The passenger list further included James Nisbet, a well-known and respected publisher and reporter. And then there was Roseanna Keenan, a notorious San Francisco madam, with seven of her "employees." Mrs. Keenan was going to Victoria, where her husband owned the Fashion Hotel, which had a music hall with a bar where her "employees" would be entertaining the mostly male customers.

An artist's rendition of *Brother Jonathan* steaming over rolling ocean swells with sails set. SAN FRANCISCO MARITIME NATIONAL HISTORIC PARK, DORIS CHASE COLLECTION

North of Point Bonita, powerful headwinds combined with a big rolling swell to slow the ship. She constantly took green water over her bow and along her decks. Her walking-beam engine and steam boilers, driving the two large paddlewheels, worked overtime to keep the ship moving north. Deckhands occasionally had to brave the elements outside to check on equipment or to stand lookout. The passengers, however, most of whom were seasick, stayed dry inside.

For two days, *Brother Jonathan* crawled north, fighting for every mile of sea. By midday on Sunday, when she was close to the California-Oregon border, the seas had built up so high that the ship could not maintain forward motion. Soon after that, Captain De Wolf accepted that the storm was beyond his ship's capability and turned back, planning to take shelter in nearby Crescent City, California, until conditions improved. A light mist hung over the land, though visibility at sea was said to be about two miles.

All captains on the route understood the coastal dangers and were well aware of the locations of all the hazards. De Wolf was no exception. He had sailed the west coast for many years, and he knew he was in the vicinity of St. George's Reef, also known as the Dragon's Teeth. That vicious semicircle of potential destruction stands out from the land for some six miles.

Captain De Wolf was on the bridge and monitoring the navigation and conditions, but neither he nor his quartermaster, or the lookouts, if they were posted, noticed *Brother Jonathan* was closing in on the deadly reef. As the ship approached disaster with every passing second, rolling with the big swells, apparently no one on board saw the surf over the rocks until it was far too late. As she rolled fore and aft and from side to side in concert with the aggressive waves, the ship's bow was lifted up and over the rocks before the bottom of her hull crunched down. A subsequent swell lifted her again and pushed her even farther forward. De Wolf called for full astern, but the ship was caught and would not move. Her bottom was torn out by the impact, and as a result of the shock, the mainmast broke free and pierced the decks like a spear. It only stopped its destructive descent when the stout yardarm caught on an obstruction. A few minutes later, as the ship rolled and ground its hull on the rocks, another swell lifted her again, only to drop her with a "tremendous thump." That was followed by part of the broken keel surfacing on one side. *Brother Jonathan* was barely afloat. The only thing keeping her from sliding into the depths was the jagged rock embedded in her belly.

Accepting that *Brother Jonathan* and all those on board were in extreme danger, Captain De Wolf gave the order to abandon ship—easier said than done, especially on a rolling and jerking ship that was being pounded by high waves. Getting the passengers and crew off the doomed ship was a nightmare, even though officers and crew worked fast to get passengers into cork life preservers and to release the lifeboats. One was launched from the windward side, but too many panic-stricken male passengers jumped in the overloaded boat, which rolled almost immediately. None survived the cold waters and surf crashing on the rocks, although one man did cling to the upturned craft for a while.

The first officer loaded a wooden lifeboat with women and lowered it on the lee, or starboard side. The constant movement of the ship caused the lifeboat to swing violently. It crashed its bow into *Brother Jonathan* and was smashed, spilling its human cargo into the sea. Some were rescued, but only temporarily. On the windward side of the ship, Third Officer James Patterson and the steward, David Farrell, had four women and three children in their lifeboat, in addition to five men. As it was being lowered, another woman and a baby were taken aboard. That boat reached the sea safely, despite having one side damaged when the ship almost rolled on it. Patterson and his men pulled hard on the oars, swinging their fragile boat around the stern of the stranded ship and heading through the white-capped waves for dry land. They were the only ones to successfully leave the ship. Even so, they still had a tremendous fight ahead if they were to reach shore safely.

A few minutes after the two crewmen and their passengers left the ship, while the lifeboat was hidden from sight in a trough between the waves, *Brother Jonathan* broke apart and sank. She went down roughly 45 minutes after she hit the reef. The captain and the army officers, plus their wives and far too many others, went down with the ship. Those in the lifeboat handled by Patterson and Farrell were the only survivors. After a hard time rowing the damaged lifeboat in the surf, they found their way ashore in Oregon's uninhabited Chetco Harbour. From there, after their valiant struggle for survival, they walked another eight miles to Crescent City to find shelter and tell their tale of the tragedy.

Over the next days and weeks, bodies drifted ashore from the wreck. Some were identifiable, many were not. The sea had stripped their clothes from them, and the action of waves upon rocks had obliterated personal distinguishing features from many. One hundred and seventy people died because *Brother Jonathan* hit St. George's Reef. Fewer than 75 bodies were recovered. Only 16 men, women and children lived.

In 1993, 128 years after the tragedy, a salvage company, Deep Sea Research, calculated that the ship had not sunk beside the reef. Instead, it had drifted like a grotesque paddle-wheel-powered submarine through the water on its way to the seabed and ended up two miles away. The company sent a mini-sub down to the location and found the remains of the ship in 275 feet of water. Three years later, another mini-sub discovered a fortune in gold coins in the vicinity. Hundreds of other artifacts were brought to the surface, but no more human remains were found.

CHAPTER

3

Alaskan's Last Voyage

THE HUGE SIDEWHEEL STEAMER *ALASKAN* was built in the summer of 1883 at Chester, Pennsylvania, for use on the Columbia River and Puget Sound. *Alaskan* was one of two similar iron-hulled ships built for and owned by financier, businessman and journalist Henry Villard. She was 276 feet long with a beam of 39.6 feet and had a main hold depth of 14.5 feet. She weighed 1,718 tons and was rigged as an auxiliary schooner.

In 1884, Villard owned the Oregon Railway and Navigation Company. The design of his two sidewheelers was based on that of similar ships working between ports on Chesapeake Bay. They were intended to be inland ships, not designed for use on open oceans. Before they could take up their assigned tasks, however, they had to navigate the South Atlantic Ocean, the Straits of Magellan and the Pacific coasts of South and Central America before reaching the dreaded Columbia River bar. Despite being designed for use in calm water, both ships made the long voyage over big ocean swells apparently without significant damage. It wasn't until they were safely inside the boundaries of Oregon's rivers that their deficiencies came to light.

Alaskan's debut on the Columbia River was far from auspicious. She was simply too big to navigate any farther upstream than Portland, so she was reduced to running hard between that city and Astoria, on the coast, in competition with the vessels of other companies. *Alaskan* also burned more coal than originally calculated, which made her more expensive to run. After a few years of unprofitable service, the company transferred her to Puget Sound. There, at least, the waters were deep enough for her to service the route from Tacoma to Seattle, Port Townsend and across Juan de Fuca Strait to Victoria. Much of the time, too, the waters were less boisterous than the open oceans.

A year later, *Alaskan* needed maintenance work done on her hull. Because there were no facilities big enough for her in Puget Sound or at Vancouver Island ports, she was sent to San Francisco.

Ordinarily, a ship being sent on a relatively long voyage would carry freight and, if possible, a few passengers to offset running costs. *Alaskan* might have carried some paying traffic on her run from Tacoma to her home port of Portland, but when she left there on the morning of Saturday, May 11, 1889, she was in ballast with no passengers on board, although there were erroneous reports to the contrary. Her complement was just 34 persons, under the command of Captain R.E. Howes.

Alaskan crossed the notorious Columbia River bar safely and set course for San Francisco. Her cruising speed for the southbound journey was said to be nine knots, and her initial course took her 18 miles offshore. By 11:00 p.m. she was closer in, no more than 14 miles out at sea. She passed the Yaquina Head lighthouse in reasonably good weather—just a light wind and occasional rain showers. According to the ship's barometer, there was no hint of any drastic change, but change was coming anyway.

On Sunday the winds picked up, and soon the waves began to build and to break. *Alaskan* had a hard time maintaining seaway as the Pacific took on a stormy aspect. In heavy seas, sidewheel steamers waddle like ducks and geese. They look ungainly and are difficult to control. *Alaskan* was no exception. Big, rolling waves slowed her to a crawl. The seas broke over her bow and washed her decks. The paddlewheels had trouble keeping her moving.

By the middle of the afternoon, *Alaskan* was 18 miles west of Cape Blanco and in real trouble. The heavy seas made the ship roll from side to side, alternately lifting first one paddlewheel clear of the water and then the

This painting by an unknown artist shows *Alaskan* fighting for survival in her final storm. *LEWIS & DRYDEN'S MARINE HISTORY OF THE PACIFIC NORTHWEST*, PORTLAND, 1895

other. The ship, hardly making any headway, was impossible to control.

Although her hull was made of iron, *Alaskan's* decks and upper works were constructed from wood. The relentless pounding by the seas gradually pulled the after cabin apart, tearing its anchoring bolts through the deck planking. As more and more holes appeared and sea water poured in, the crew risked their lives on the slippery, rolling deck to stuff blankets and other soft materials into the holes to keep the water out. It was a valiant effort, but the sidewheel steamer was being systematically destroyed by the sea. In an attempt to maintain some stability, the captain ordered his crew to rig an emergency staysail. It was a gesture, little more.

At about 6:00 p.m., a large wave smashed into the port paddlewheel structure and tore it away, leaving the wheel damaged and exposed. By then, Captain Howes knew his ship had little time left. Sea water poured in, flooding the holds. The crew worked the pumps for hours, but the water crept higher and higher until it put out the fires. The boilers cooled down, and the ship fell dark and silent, except for the wrenching of wood against metal and the sound of water streaming in from dozens of holes.

Concerned for the safety of his crew, Captain Howes ordered the boats to be lowered and loaded most of the crew into them. Someone saw lights from another ship and fired two distress rockets as they were leaving. The crew managed to get three boats away, all with personnel on board, and towed them behind the ship in single file. Now only the captain and four of his crew remained on board, including the quartermaster. He was somehow washed overboard into the open paddlewheel, which would still have been turning slowly with the action of the ship and sea, and was terribly injured. Although he was later recovered from the water, he died soon after.

As midnight passed and with no rescue in sight, the situation appeared hopeless for the captain and the three men still on board *Alaskan*. Sea conditions prevented them being taken off by the lifeboats, and the ship was disintegrating under them. At 1:00 a.m. on Monday, Captain Howes released the towline to prevent his lifeboats being pulled under when *Alaskan* sank—as she most certainly would do, and soon.

The distress rockets had been seen by a distant tug towing a heavy barge. *Vigilante* (or possibly *Vigilant*) could not release her manned tow without endangering its crew, so could only rumble toward the sinking ship at slow speed.

Alaskan slid beneath the waves at about 2:30 a.m., long before the tug arrived. By this time, the lifeboats had become separated, and those on board could no longer see the foundering ship. The captain and chief engineer saved themselves by using a piece of wooden decking as a raft. It was unstable and would have been washed by waves every few seconds, but it was better than nothing. Seeing the pilothouse floating nearby with other men riding it, the chief engineer tried to swim to the larger debris but failed and was never seen again.

When *Vigilante* arrived on the scene sometime Monday evening, its crew found Captain Howes still clinging to his makeshift raft and just as desperately to life. One of the crew was reported to have been picked up by a British barque en route to Hong Kong and was landed there at the end of the voyage. The tug also rescued men from one of the boats. A second boat reached shore safely, but the third disappeared without a trace.

The steamer *Columbia,* on course from San Francisco to Astoria, Oregon, met the tug near the scene of the disaster and took the few members of *Alaskan*'s crew on board. Only 16 out of the 34 who sailed on *Alaskan* survived, and they owed their lives to the captain's decision to put them in the lifeboats early.

The SS *Columbia* was destined to meet her own catastrophic end on the same stretch of coastline 18 years later.

4

Eliza Anderson:
Aground in Alaska

PERHAPS THE STRANGEST STORY ABOUT ships working the long, dangerous coastline from California to Alaska would be that of the old inland sidewheel steamship *Eliza Anderson*. Although she served her succession of owners for 40 years, working hard on short hauls between a long list of northwest ports, she was not a happy ship, nor was she a safe one toward the end of her life.

Eliza Anderson was built by Samuel Farman's yard in Portland, Oregon, and launched on November 27, 1858. Built of wood and powered by side paddlewheels driven by "a low pressure boiler generating steam for a single cylinder walking-beam steam engine," she was 197 feet long and 25.5 feet in beam. As usual with paddle steamers, she was relatively light in weight, being rated at only 276 tons capacity.

She departed on her maiden voyage on January 2, 1859, making trial runs up and down the Willamette and Columbia rivers. In March of the same year, after being sold to a consortium of Pacific Northwest businessmen and steamboat operators, she steamed up the coasts of Oregon and Washington, through Juan de Fuca Strait and past Race Rocks into Victoria. At that time, Vancouver Island (on which Victoria stands) had just been designated a separate British colony from mainland British Columbia.

Eliza Anderson went to work almost immediately, making a run from Victoria through the San Juans and the Gulf Islands and up the Fraser River to Fort Langley. She plied her trade between the two ports until the end of June. Early in July, she set out to tow a sternwheeler from Victoria to Gray's Harbor, Washington. Due to mechanical problems on the sternwheeler while in Juan de Fuca Strait, the two ships had to put back into Esquimalt. *Eliza Anderson* left the sternwheeler there and carried a contingent of miners from Victoria down to Olympia, her first voyage into Puget Sound. The following month, she began service on the mail run between Olympia and Victoria, making regularly scheduled calls at 10 ports en route.

For the next few months, *Eliza Anderson* was shuttled back and forth between the Olympia–Victoria route and the Fraser River run from Victoria to Fort Langley. In early

November, Captain Wright placed his ship on a regular weekly schedule that took her from Olympia to Victoria and on to New Westminster, a Fraser River port, and then back on the same route. An advertisement in the Olympia, Washington, *Pioneer Democrat* newspaper for a voyage on the *Eliza Anderson* read:

United States Mail Line

From

Olympia to Semiahmoo.

The new and splendid steamer

Eliza Anderson,

Thos. Wright, Commander,

Will hereafter leave Olympia every Monday morning at 7 o'clock for STEILACOOM, SEATTLE, PORT MADISON, PORT GAMBLE, PORT LUDLOW, PORT TOWNSEND, WHIDBY'S ISLAND, NEW DUNGINESS, BELLINGHAM BAY, SAN JUAN ISLANDS and VICTORIA, V.I.

The *Eliza Anderson* has been recently refitted, and now offers superior accommodations for passengers. Her freighting capacity has been enlarged, and cattle, produce, &c., will be carried at REDUCED PRICES.

For further particulars, address, JOHN H. SCRANTON,

Olympia, May 4, 1860.

Just prior to the American Civil War, and therefore long before the civil rights movement began in the south in 1955, *Eliza Anderson* was inadvertently mixed up in a

The sidewheel steamer *Eliza Anderson* on the Alaskan coast in 1898.
UNIVERSITY OF WASHINGTON TRANSPORTATION DIGITAL COLLECTION TRA0306

racial dispute. Charles Mitchell, a 14-year-old black slave, ran away from his owner in Olympia, Washington, and stowed away on board *Eliza Anderson* in September 1860. Mitchell was hoping to get to Canada and gain his freedom. He was discovered while the ship was at a Puget Sound port and only managed to remain aboard because he persuaded one of the crew to let him work his passage to Victoria. None of the ship's officers, apparently, had any idea of the arrangement. Unfortunately, the acting governor of Washington territory was on board with his family. When he heard of the situation, he ordered the boy locked in a cabin when the ship was a few miles south of Victoria.

Thanks to the intervention of Victoria's concerned citizens, both black and white, a Canadian court freed Mitchell, against the wishes of the acting governor and *Eliza Anderson*'s skipper at the time, Captain John Fleming. In the convoluted legalese wording of the time, the captain issued a strongly worded protest against the court order:

> Whereas, a negro boy called Charles, the property of James Tilton, Esq., of Olympia, Washington Territory, did on the 24th inst., run away from his master, and secrete himself on board this vessel, and upon the fact being made known to the undersigned, the said negro was placed in [the] charge of one of the officers of the ship, that he might be returned to his master; and Whereas, upon the arrival of the ship at Victoria, a writ of *habeas corpus* was issued by Chief Justice Cameron and placed in the hands of the Sheriff of Victoria, who demanded of the undersigned the delivery of the said negro, and upon the refusal of the undersigned to deliver the said negro the said sheriff threatened to force open the room in which the negro was confined on board of said vessel, whereupon the undersigned, to prevent the destruction of property, and in all probability much bloodshed, opened the door of said room, and upon doing so, the sheriff took the negro from on board the vessel.
>
> Now therefore, the undersigned protests against the whole proceedings as illegal and a breach of international law, and demands the immediate delivery of the said negro, Charles, that he may be restored to his master.
>
> John R. Fleming, Captain, U.S.M. Steamer *Eliza Anderson*.

Fleming's protest failed to move the Canadian court. Charles Mitchell was allowed to stay in Victoria as a free man.

Eliza Anderson remained on the Olympia–Victoria route until it was no longer profitable. After a lay up in Olympia for an unspecified amount of time, she was overhauled and sent on a series of voyages into Alaskan waters on the Inside Passage, venturing as far as Wrangell Island. In 1877 she was sent to Seattle and decommissioned. She was there for six years, during which time she sank at her moorings. Re-enter Captain Wright. He had her raised from the silt, pumped out and cleaned thoroughly. She then went back into his service, this time on the Seattle–New Westminster route.

By 1890 the aging sidewheel steamer was laid up again. Her latest berth was on the Duwamish River, Washington, where she was used as a gambling hall, among other non-nautical functions. The Yukon gold rush of 1896 changed her luck one more time.

With untold numbers demanding passage to Alaska in order to ascend the Yukon River to the Klondike, *Eliza Anderson* and a bevy of equally ancient steamers were pressed into service. One was a sternwheeler, which was intended for the voyage up the Yukon River to the Klondike. Known as "floating coffins," which they surely were, the fleet of five decrepit vessels took on passengers and departed Seattle for Alaska on August 10, 1897. Their initial destination was St. Michael, on the west coast at the Yukon River delta. The talk along the Seattle waterfront was that the

Old Anderson, to use her nickname, was unseaworthy and had not a hope of reaching her destination.

The ships in the convoy were *Eliza Anderson*, 39 years old; a steam tug, *Richard Holyoke*, 20 years old, which was towing the three other vessels; a sternwheeler, *W.K. Merwin*, 14 years old; a coal barge, *Politkosky* (formerly a Russian gunboat, hence the name), of unknown vintage; and a yachting schooner, *William J. Bryant*, owned by a wealthy playboy.

The hastily put together plan was quite straightforward: steam in convoy to St. Michael. Four of the ships would be left there, and all the passengers would continue up the Yukon River on *W.K. Merwin*, the sternwheeler. Of course, greed, in the guise of taking on more passengers than the ships could legally carry, created problems. Space per passenger was severely limited, and passengers and crew got into brawls with each other.

The fleet stopped to take on coal for the fires at Comox, halfway up the east coast of Vancouver Island. The next scheduled stop, also for coal, was at Kodiak, Alaska. The voyage up the coast did not endear *Eliza Anderson* to all her passengers. Five out of the forty or so on board got off in Kodiak, too concerned for their own safety to continue. Their fear was well placed, as the worst part of the voyage was still to come. Ahead was the notoriously stormy Bering Sea. Before that challenge, however, there was another stop on the timetable: Dutch Harbor in the Aleutian Islands.

For *Eliza Anderson*, there was another problem: her

crew, who were supposed to have loaded the bunkers with coal at Kodiak, had cheated the ship's owners and their officers. They also had risked the lives of all on board. Instead of hauling sack after sack of the coal aboard for fuel, many of the men had slacked off and hidden the coal sacks. Consequently, when the steamer sailed away from Kodiak, she did not have enough fuel to reach the Aleutian Islands.

Soon after leaving Kodiak, a storm separated *Eliza Anderson* from the rest of the fleet. It wasn't difficult to do. The ship had run out of coal, and therefore the engine had threatened to stop. Passengers and crew worked together to tear wooden fittings apart and burn anything combustible to get the ship back to land for more coal. The captain for this northern voyage, Thomas Powers, coaxed his ship back to Kodiak Island, where they moored in front of a small abandoned cannery. There, just waiting to be taken away, was 75 tons of coal. That was just enough to get them to Dutch Harbor, on Unalaska Island, the main port in the Aleutians, where the other ships waited.

Eliza Anderson had been reported missing in the storm; consequently, the US Revenue cutter *Corwin*, on its annual Bering Sea patrol, went in search of the ship, found her somewhere between the Aleutians and Kodiak Island and escorted her to Dutch Harbor. But *Eliza Anderson*'s troubles were far from over. While coming into port, she collided with a dock and sustained damage. When a steam pipe burst, the remaining passengers on board had had enough. They refused to go any farther in the unseaworthy vessel and went ashore. There they joined another ship heading north.

Eliza Anderson was destined never to return to her Puget Sound ports. She remained at anchor in Dutch Harbor throughout that winter until a storm took her from the mooring and drove her up on a beach. There she began to break apart. The *Seattle Post-Intelligencer* newspaper reported the loss on March 31, 1898:

> The old *Eliza Anderson,* after an interesting career of 40 years, is at last a total wreck. During a terrible storm early in March she broke from her anchorage at Dutch Harbor and went ashore before any assistance could be given her. She is now lying on her side, with the tide ebbing and flowing through several jagged holes in her bottom. She will surely and slowly go to pieces. The news of the *Anderson*'s wreck was brought to Seattle by the steamer *Bertha* . . . The wreck in the far north is a fitting end to the steamer, which has several times been rescued from the boneyard and put back into commission.

It wasn't much of an epitaph, considering the ship's history, but at least the old sidewheeler's demise had been reported with a certain amount of compassion. *Eliza Anderson* was left there in the North, on a barren beach in the storm-swept Aleutian Islands, until she completely disintegrated.

5

City of Rio de Janeiro: Death at the Golden Gate

THE SS *CITY OF RIO DE JANEIRO* was an iron-hulled steamship of 4,548 tons built at Chester, Pennsylvania, and launched on March 6, 1878. In addition to steam, she also was rigged with sail as a barquentine. She was designed for the United States and Brazil Mail Steamship Company for service between the US and Brazil. In 1881, she was sold to the Pacific Mail Steamship Company and made the long voyage around the southern tip of South America to the company's base in San Francisco. There she was remodelled into an ocean-going passenger ship. Her new route would be trans-Pacific, sailing between San Francisco, Honolulu, Yokohama and Hong Kong. For the next 17 years, the *City of Rio de Janeiro* crossed and recrossed the North Pacific Ocean with passengers and cargo, although not without incident.

In the summer of 1890, while in Hong Kong's busy harbour, she was in a collision with the British-registered ship *Bombay* and suffered considerable damage. She had to be repaired there before she could attempt another ocean crossing. In 1895, she was in trouble again when she ran up on a reef outside Nagasaki, Japan, and tore a large hole in her hull. Two years later, she was almost lost when she was caught by a typhoon between Japan and Hawaii.

For a time during the Spanish-American War, in 1898, the steam barquentine was leased to the US government as a troopship, carrying soldiers from San Francisco to Manila, in the Philippines. At the end of those hostilities, the *City of Rio de Janeiro* returned to her previously assigned route to Asia. Her personnel consisted of American officers and a predominantly Chinese crew, many of the latter knowing little or no English. The Americans, with the exception of a bilingual boatswain, were equally ignorant of the Chinese language.

By the turn of the century, the *City of Rio de Janeiro* was into her third decade of long-distance service. In those many years, she had survived storms and high seas. She had carried thousands of passengers across a vast ocean, and she had landed them all safely, either in Hawaii, Asia or America. She was a ship that passengers felt they could depend on, but her machinery was getting old and was subject to breakdowns.

The steam barquentine's captain, William Ward, was a veteran of the trans-Pacific run and had been in command of the *City of Rio de Janeiro* for almost four years, although he was only 38 years old. In port, especially his home port of San Francisco, he was a popular and charming dinner guest at the homes of the wealthy. He was reported to have said that in the event of an accident, he would go down with his ship. That possibly tongue-in-cheek comment would prove to be prophetic.

There were at least 210 people on board for the *City of Rio de Janeiro*'s first eastbound voyage of 1901. Two hundred and ten people left Hong Kong on January 19 with no idea that many of them were embarking on their final sea voyage. In the cargo holds, the ship carried 2,423 sheets of pig tin (99 percent pure tin), 1,800 rolls of grass mats, 1,750 bales of hemp, plus silk, tea, sugar, 200 sacks of mail and assorted general cargo. The crossing was made difficult by bad weather and plagued by mechanical problems. Consequently, the *City of Rio de Janeiro* was running three days late when she dropped anchor off the California coast at Point Lobos to wait for a San Francisco Bay pilot. It was late afternoon on February 21, 1901, and thick fog enveloped the ship and obscured the land.

The pilot, Captain Frederick Jordan, came aboard from a cutter at 5:00 p.m. Jordan had guided hundreds of ships through the Golden Gate and safely into port during his 12 or more years as a San Francisco pilot. He knew the waters intimately and understood the regular fogs. Taking the barquentine into port should have been a routine job for a man of his experience, once the fog dispersed.

The fog cleared soon after Jordan boarded the steamer. The crew hauled anchor, and the *City of Rio de Janeiro* crept forward, heading for the Golden Gate and the safe haven of her home port. A few minutes later the fog closed in again, and they had to anchor once more.

On board the ship, the most important passenger, US Consul General to Hong Kong Rounsevelle Wildman, was getting upset. He and his family had an important engagement to attend in Washington, DC—the inauguration of President McKinley—and sitting on a ship in a fog just outside San Francisco was not his idea of time well spent. He began working on the captain over dinner that night to get the ship moving, in spite of the fog, and end the voyage as soon as possible. Wildman's diplomatic position gave him many privileges and valuable contacts; he was powerful and persuasive. Captain Ward, who had earlier stated in public that there was no way he was taking his ship through the narrows in thick fog, began to weaken. Meiggs Wharf, where the passengers would disembark, was only five miles away. To add to that, he had an invitation for a special social event on Nob Hill that night, which he did not want to miss. His presence at the function would be good for his career and would keep the company he worked for in the forefront of the minds of those wealthy enough to travel on his ocean-going passenger ship.

Company policy required ships' masters to take all due

precautions to ensure the safety of the ship, passengers, crew and cargo. Entering the Golden Gate in thick fog would not have been considered a safe enterprise. Less than eight years before, the Pacific Mail Steamship Company had lost the 3,019-ton SS *City of New York* when she was wrecked on Point Bonita, at the north side of the entrance to the Golden Gate. Captain Ward would have been well aware of that disaster.

At just before 4 a.m. the next morning, with the thick fog showing little sign of dispersing and the captain not yet on the bridge, pilot Jordan is reported to have ordered the anchor raised and the engines started. Captain Ward arrived on deck minutes later, still in his pyjamas, but left the pilot in charge of the final few miles into port. The fog cleared momentarily, perhaps from a passing wind, then closed in again. Most of the passengers and many of the crew were still asleep in their quarters. Down in the engine room amidships, the chief engineer, Philip Herlihy, answered the order from the bridge, and the engines bellowed into life.

Although the majority of the passengers remained in their cabins, oblivious to the tremble of the engines, the tail end of an all-night card game in one lounge kept four players awake at the smoky table. In the first passenger lounge, a few early risers sipped scalding coffee and talked of meeting for dinner someday soon in San Francisco.

On land, at Point Lobos, John Hyslop, the coast watcher, heard or saw the steamer raise her anchor and immediately telephoned the Merchant's Exchange, plus the US Customs and Immigration Services, to advise that a big ship was due in shortly. Hyslop noted that the fog was getting thicker. He recorded the time of his messages as 4:42 a.m.

With engines running at half speed, the ship moved cautiously through the grey world ahead. On the foredeck, crewman Frederick Lindstrom was on lookout. Peering into the fog, all he could see was grey. There were no colours and no other tones—just grey all around. That changed suddenly and dramatically. A white and red light winked at him from close ahead. Instinctively, he knew the ship was about to run aground, but he had no time to sound the alarm. The *City of Rio de Janeiro* crunched up onto a reef at the south side of the Golden Gate at 5:30 a.m. She had crossed the ocean safely only to run aground almost within hailing distance of her destination.

The impact ripped open the bottom of the hull for most of its length. Faced with such catastrophic damage and without watertight bulkheads, the ship's engine room and cargo holds flooded quickly. Only a couple of minutes after she struck, there was 10 feet of water in the forward hold. Amidships she was flooded to twice that depth, and even more coursed through to the stern. The ship was in imminent danger of sliding backwards off the rocks and sinking.

Captain Ward and other officers did their best to rouse the passengers from their cabins and get them on deck. He and Third Officer J.C. Holland then worked together to shepherd the frightened people into lifeboats.

Although attempts were made to launch the life-boats, they were mostly unsuccessful due to the language barrier between the English-speaking officers and Chinese-speaking crew; however, some boats—maybe two or three—did get away. Consul Wildman got into a lifeboat with an officer and six Chinese crewmen on the oars. His wife and son followed slowly down a rope ladder with the pilot, Frederick Jordan. As they descended, the ship lurched violently and Jordan was thrown off the ladder. It's probable that Mrs. Wildman and her son were also thrown off, as they were never seen again.

The lifeboat launching was too late for most on board. *City of Rio de Janeiro* slid beneath the waves about 18 minutes after she rammed the California rocks. Wildman's boat was cut in half by one of the ship's booms as it fell, and most of those on board, including Wildman, were either killed outright or drowned. Another lifeboat was shattered by the aft mast as the ship keeled over. A third lifeboat and its passengers only escaped the falling mast by the heroic rowing efforts of the men at the oars. With the noise of explosive air being released from within, and the sound of rending timbers combined with the screaming of tortured metal, the barquentine turned on her side and drifted down into the deeps to settle on the seabed some 320 feet below.

Pilot Jordan was sucked down with the vortex from the ship, but was able to struggle clear and reach the surface. He survived by clinging to drifting wreckage. J.C. Holland survived too. Like Jordan, he was pulled down with the ship but managed to take hold of a cork life preserver and swim up with it. He was eventually rescued by an Italian fisherman. He later told of his last sight of Captain Ward. The two officers had been walking quickly aft on the starboard side when the ship sank. Holland lived, but Captain Ward went to the seabed with his ship.

Of the 210 people on board, only 82 were saved. It was rumoured that the ship carried gold and silver bullion, but this was never noted on her cargo manifest. Possibly the cargo of 2,423 sheets of shiny tin, each weighing 107 pounds, had provoked that rumour.

The fog was so thick when *City of Rio de Janeiro* hit the semi-submerged reef that no one on shore saw the accident or heard the ship hit. Hyslop didn't, and the keeper of the Fort Point Lifeboat Station, no more than a few hundred yards from the wreck site, had no idea a ship had run ashore on his patch of coastline until a lifeboat was seen coming out of the fog two hours after the ship went down. Although rescue boats were sent out as soon as the news came in, and Italian fishermen were in the area, they found very few survivors. Other than those in the lifeboats, the few fortunate souls taken to shore from the sea that day were discovered clinging to pieces of wreckage and praying for a miracle.

It's just possible that a few unknown hardy souls survived the wreck and clung to floating debris. Unseen in the fog, they could have drifted away from the coast during the day. If they did, any hope they had of being rescued would have faded when heavy rains lashed the Golden Gate region that night, combined with building seas.

On February 24, 1901, the *New York Times* reported, "Small boats have hovered around the scene of the wreck for the past twenty-four hours, and bodies are frequently seen floating in and out with the tides, but the roughness of the water greatly hinders the work of recovery."

While Captain Ward was ultimately responsible for the tragedy, part of that responsibility should perhaps have been shared by Wildman for his insistence on getting into port, and by Jordan, who should have ensured the ship remained at anchor until weather conditions improved.

In a macabre epilogue to the tragedy, the bodies of crew and passengers were carried ashore near Fort Point by currents for years afterwards. What was left of Captain Ward's body was found there in 1903, the skeletal remains identified by the watch chain attached to his rib cage. As late as 1917, a wooden barrel with *City of Rio de Janeiro* emblazoned on it was found off Point Lobos. Two years later, more wreckage came to light in Suisun Bay, roughly 40 miles from where the ship went down.

The *City of Rio de Janeiro* lies on the seabed amidst the remains of a profusion of other ships that also misjudged the entrance to the Golden Gate. Her exact location has never been determined, and due to the number of wrecks off that part of the California coast, it probably never will be.

CHAPTER

6

Islander and
the Iceberg

CAPTAINS AND CREWS OF SHIPS working the Inside Passage
between Skagway, Alaska, and southern ports such as
Vancouver, Victoria and Seattle were well aware of the
physical limitations and peculiarities of their route. In
some places, particularly in Alaska's Lynn Canal, the seaway narrowed to less than 10 miles wide. It was known for
occasional drifting ice, regular fogs and frequently stormy
weather. It also harboured semi-submerged reefs. Company
instructions to captains stressed the need for caution in
inclement weather. Schedules, however, had to be maintained as much as possible. Often that meant travelling at
full speed to make up for delays in port. Under such conditions, accidents were almost inevitable.

The SS *Islander* was built in Glasgow, Scotland, in 1888 expressly for service on the Inside Passage between Vancouver/Victoria and Skagway. Owned by the Canadian Pacific Steam Navigation Company, she was 1,519 tons, with two funnels, two masts and twin screws and had a top speed of 15 knots. She was 240 feet long and judged by her wealthy passengers to be the most luxurious steamer on the Inside Passage.

Starting from Victoria, *Islander* had completed a few runs to Alaska and back in the summer of 1901. On August 14 of that year, she hummed with activity at the Skagway dock as millions of dollars' worth of cargo was loaded— reports spoke of $6 million in gold bullion on the manifest. Her passengers chatted happily as they made their way up the gangplanks and found their way through the corridors to their assigned cabins. The gold was said to have been stowed in a locker in the bow on the port side, with two Mounties to guard it. On the bridge, Captain Hamilton Foote and his deck officers prepared for the long haul to the south. Deep in the bowels of the ship, the engineers and stokers had the fires burning and the boilers steaming. They too were ready for departure. When the time came for the order "Cast off for'ward," followed by three short blasts on the steam whistle and "Cast off aft," the crew hauled in the mooring lines and coiled them neatly.

Among the full load of passengers were the usual complement of miners, prospectors and businessmen. One was

Islander at an Alaskan port during one of her regular summer voyages between Victoria and Skagway. LIBRARY AND ARCHIVES CANADA C009576

Charles Keating, a well-known multi-millionaire and a director of the Canadian Bank of Commerce. He was travelling with two of his sons. Also on board were Mrs. James Ross and her daughter. James Ross, who did not sail on that voyage, was then commissioner of the Yukon Territory. Additionally, Peter Warren Wentworth Bell, a retired chief factor of the Hudson's Bay Company, was on board. He had been travelling in the Yukon with a Dr. John Duncan, and they were on their way home to Victoria.

Ice had been reported drifting in the narrow confines of Lynn Canal, yet that warning failed to induce the captain to slow his ship. Steaming down Lynn Canal, north of Juneau, in the early hours of the following morning, the ship's steam whistle was sounded loudly at least three times, trying to pick up echoes from any obstructions ahead. It was standard practice but did not always work. On this voyage, the inevitable happened.

There were rumours that Captain Foote and the Lynn Canal pilot were at odds, the captain having reprimanded the pilot for being under the influence of alcohol. Whether that verbal altercation or the pilot's condition had anything to do with the events of the next few minutes is unknown. *Islander* slammed into an iceberg, a large drifting remnant from the icefields of Glacier Bay. (This was 11 years before another iceberg would sink the mighty *Titanic* in the North Atlantic.) The collision ripped the port quarter open, and the ship's speed hastened the entry of the frigid waters into her forward compartments.

Islander began to go down by the bow even as the crew desperately tried to steer her to Douglas Island, the closest land. Within five minutes, as she drifted helplessly with the outbound tide, her bow had sunk so far that her propellers and rudder were clear of the water and therefore useless for propulsion or steering. According to the later testimony of surviving passengers, the accident showed the ship's officers and crew to have been less than professional in their attitude toward those in their care.

Passenger Charles Ross was in bed, as were many others on the ship. He and his wife, Minnie, felt the shock of the impact with the ice, got up and looked out the cabin door. A passing officer told him there was "nothing the matter." A few minutes afterwards, he heard chopping sounds as some crew members tried to break through jammed cabin doors to free passengers. Mr. Ross dressed and went on deck, where he discovered that one lifeboat, designed to carry 40 people, had already left the ship, but with only 8 crew members aboard. Ross ran back to his cabin and told his wife to dress quickly and get on deck. At this time, it appears that no one had given the order to abandon ship, and no one called the passengers from their cabins, including the ones with recently damaged doors, but the crew were leaving anyway.

One of the lifeboats narrowly missed being cut in two when it went too close to the still-spinning propeller as the stern rose. When Mr. and Mrs. Ross reached the outer deck, they saw that the last lifeboat had left the sinking ship but was close enough to hail. Ross yelled at the crew to return and take them off, but his plea for help was ignored. The couple put on life preservers and went into the icy cold waters as the ship settled under them. No more than 15 minutes after she hit the ice, *Islander* stood on her nose and plunged to the seabed 175 feet below.

As *Islander* went under, there were reports of an explosion from within the ship, almost certainly the result of air pressure blowing out the main windows, plus possibly the reaction of hot boilers to the sudden incursion of cold water.

The "explosion" created a deadly barrage of wood splinters and other flying debris that viciously attacked the passengers struggling in the water.

Charles Ross caught hold of a piece of wreckage and clung to it for over three bone-chilling hours before being picked up. He never saw his wife alive again. Minnie Ross' body was found drifting in the debris field.

Considering the ship was said to be full, with at least 120 passengers and 62 crew, it is surprising that only 40 lives were lost. Of those, 16 were crew, including Captain Foote, and the remainder were passengers.

Salvage attempts began soon after the ship went down. The hull was located in 1902, but despite many attempts, it was not until over three decades later that it was raised. After two seasons of intense effort by a team of salvage experts, *Islander*'s hull broke the surface on July 20, 1934. It was filled with accumulated silt from being on the seabed for so many years, but that was expected by the team. The most serious discovery was that the bow section, where the iceberg had hit, was missing. Instead of the "gaping hole" that had been expected, 60 feet of the bow had disappeared, apparently "sheared off." That bow section was where the gold had been stored in a locker, according to the RCMP constables assigned to guard it.

What was left of the purser's office, located amidships, was cleaned out, and gold nuggets and gold dust were recovered to the disappointingly low value of approximately

$75,000. It was far less than anticipated, based on the reported $6 million that had been taken aboard. Spurred on by thoughts of the gold, salvage companies renewed their efforts to locate the large bow section. Ninety-five years after *Islander* plummeted to the bottom of Lynn Canal, the bow section was finally located by a team of underwater archaeologists, appropriately perhaps, from the MV *Jolly Roger*.

The gold, said to be worth about $100 million in today's markets, has yet to be found and rescued from its resting place in the silt among other relics of the wreck of the *Islander*. Perhaps it never will be recovered.

7

Columbia:
Speed Kills

THE DISTANCE BY SEA BETWEEN Portland, Oregon, and San Francisco is just over 900 miles. For a vessel as dependable as the SS *Columbia*, that represented no more than 10 hours of steaming. The 27-year-old coastal veteran had completed over 400 round-trip voyages between the two cities. In 1889 she had carried the captain and crew of the storm-wrecked sidewheeler *Alaskan* home to Astoria. She was so dependable that only one southbound voyage had kept her at sea more than one night in the past 15 years.

Columbia was owned by the San Francisco and Portland Steamship Company, which was in turn owned by the Union Pacific Railroad. Railways ran to strict schedules, and the company's directors expected their ships to do the same. *Columbia*'s captain, Peter Doran, was well aware of the rules.

Columbia was a relatively small passenger ship of 2,721 tons. She was 309 feet long and had a beam of 38.5 feet. Her capacity was 382 passengers in first class and steerage. She normally carried a crew of 60. Built on the east coast and launched in 1880, her first voyage had been around the tip of South America and up the Pacific coastline to Portland, Oregon. She carried a heavy load of 13 railway locomotives plus 200 railway cars and associated supplies. She was, incidentally, the first vessel to use Thomas Edison's new incandescent interior lighting system.

On the latest northbound voyage, which started about midday on July 20, 1907, *Columbia* carried 189 passengers, many of whom were schoolteachers returning home from a convention in Los Angeles. She met the first of the fog just before evening set in. By midnight, when they were about 12 miles southwest of Shelter Cove, California, the fog was a thick grey mass surrounding the ship. Because of the conditions, Captain Doran had been on the bridge for a few hours. He was keeping watch, although he continued to run his ship at full speed. A lookout reported visibility as being no more than two ship lengths on either side of *Columbia*'s rails. The ship's foghorn was sounded regularly, creating an eerie illusion of danger in the clammy darkness. The lookout heard another ship's foghorn in the night and sent word to the captain; still he did not slow down. Instead, he maintained his speed and his course of north by northeast.

Seven hours earlier, the small wooden-hulled steam schooner *San Pedro* had left Eureka in northern California. Loaded with 390,000 board feet of redwood, she was heading south for San Pedro, beside the Port of Los Angeles. Her course was southeast by south. The 457-ton ship was travelling at about eight knots, which was probably not far below her top speed. At 12:15 a.m., the lookout heard a foghorn off the port bow and reported it to Ben Hendricksen, the first officer, on the bridge. Hendricksen responded by ordering a turn to starboard, without reducing speed, to give *San Pedro* more sea room. Every minute after that, he gave a warning blast to let the other ship know where he was.

On *Columbia*, Captain Doran could hear *San Pedro* clearly yet still did not slow down. Within 15 minutes, *Columbia*'s lookout saw the ghostly shape of a ship in the fog, and it was coming straight at them—no more than 50 yards away. Doran blew two blasts on the steam whistle to signal that he was passing. From *San Pedro*'s bridge, Hendricksen saw *Columbia* at about the same time. He rang down to stop engines and gave four quick, shrill blasts on his whistle as *Columbia* steamed across his bow.

Finally realizing the imminent danger, Doran ordered his ship full astern. His reaction was too late. The ship was still moving fast when *San Pedro* rammed her bluff bow into *Columbia*'s iron-plated hull, opening up a large hole

This pen-and-ink sketch by an unknown artist shows the SS *Columbia* as she looked soon after she was launched in 1880. PHOTOGRAPH COURTESY OF PGE RETIREES' ASSOCIATION, HTTP://PGERETIREES.ORG

approximately six-feet square on the starboard side and mortally wounding her.

San Pedro had also suffered considerable damage, but despite the fact that she was taking on water, her captain took a close look at the hole in *Columbia*'s side. What he saw convinced him that the larger ship was doomed, so he ordered his three boats lowered to pick up survivors. On *Columbia*, Captain Doran ordered his boats lowered too. There was no time to waste, as the ship was listing to starboard and appeared to be ready to roll over. Chief Engineer Jackson told of the noise: "All was confusion and turmoil. The roar of the water as it poured into the hole of the *Columbia*'s side was deafening."

A passenger, Otillia Leidelt, agreed: "The rush of the water into our vessel made a noise that was heard above the din of the crazed crowd."

Engineer Jackson was one of the lucky ones. His physical strength saved him, allowing him to swim away from the sinking ship. He managed to catch a line thrown from *San Pedro* and was hauled on board.

As passengers and crew struggled to get off *Columbia*, Captain Doran remained on the bridge. When his ship began her final plunge less than 10 minutes after the collision, Otillia Leidelt said that the captain had tied the ship's steam whistle open and stood by the rail with his arms outstretched. Passengers reported that he called out, "Goodbye. God bless you." That was the last seen or heard of him as *Columbia* sank.

Safe on *San Pedro*, Jackson watched in horror as the ship whose engines he had looked after went down. In an interview on shore, he said, "As she sank I could dimly see many men dash across her deck toward the *San Pedro*: the next moment the fog had hidden the dreadful scenes." Jackson also commented on the fate of the steerage passengers: "I am sure that many [of them] did not leave their staterooms, as the interval was so short between the time she was struck and the time she sank that the men had not time to get to the deck."

As passengers and crew jumped overboard and floundered in the icy waters, the strongest made for the safety of life rafts or lifeboats. Those who could climb on board or were dragged aboard by others were collected by *San Pedro*. She was listing, with much of her bow missing, but stayed afloat, no doubt due to the buoyancy of her big cargo of lumber.

In the water, there was mayhem as the cries and screams of the dying echoed through the darkness. Some women swam for safety holding children in their arms. Their efforts to save the youngsters were brave but futile; none of the children aboard *Columbia* survived the night. The efforts of a few crew members who manned some of the lifeboats saved many adults. There were heroes among the passengers too. Emma Griese had put her life jacket on backwards and so found it impossible to keep her face out of the water. She was saved by 16-year-old Maybelle Watson, who held her head above water so she could breathe.

Survivors who had been rescued and considered reasonably safe on *San Pedro*'s deck were constantly swept by waves breaking over them. When the rear mast collapsed, it knocked four people into the sea. Two were rescued for a second time, but the others were lost.

About five hours after the collision, two other ships arrived on the scene to assist with rescue efforts. They were the steamer *Roanoke* and a small coastal ship, *George W. Elder*. They helped *San Pedro* and collected *Columbia* passengers and crew who were still in the sea clinging to wreckage. One of *Columbia*'s lifeboats, carrying 18 passengers and crew, made its way to land at Shelter Cove.

When she left San Francisco, *Columbia* carried 251 people on board. Less than a day later, 88 passengers and crew members had died violent deaths.

Star of Bengal: Adrift on Coronation Island

THERE ARE FEW THINGS THAT evoke deeper feelings of sadness for mariners than the evidence of a sunken ship. There is something chilling in the sight of a mast, or more than one, poking its lonely tip above the surface of the sea. When the toll of death is counted for those who went down with the ship, the sadness becomes absolute.

The three-masted windjammer *Star of Bengal*, owned by the Alaska Packers Association, was blown ashore on the rocks of Coronation Island, southeast of Baranof Island on the Alaska panhandle, on September 20, 1908. In addition to 5,260 cases of canned salmon, she had 137 people on board at the time. Most were cannery workers heading home at the end of the season; the remaining 21 were crew.

They were all bound for San Francisco. When the *Star of Bengal* foundered in the autumn gale, she took 110 people with her to the seabed.

Star of Bengal was an iron-hulled, fully rigged ship, 262 feet long with a beam of 40 feet. Built by the famed Belfast shipyard Harland & Wolff, she was launched on January 3, 1874, and was registered at 1,870 tons.

The big windjammer was strong, and she was fast for her era. She made her maiden voyage to Australia, sailing from London to Melbourne in 81 days. A month later, she raced from Melbourne to San Francisco in 58 days. Heading for home, *Star of Bengal* took just 111 days to travel from San Francisco to Liverpool. She kept up those speeds in a gruelling annual schedule for the officers and crew for 12 years, until she was sold to a San Francisco company in the summer of 1898. From 1876 to 1886, she was in the Indian jute trade, making regular voyages between London and Calcutta, usually in a respectable average time of 96 days.

Later, before being sold, she made a few voyages to ports on the west coast of South America and as far north as San Francisco. Little is known of the eight years she spent working for the San Francisco–based company, but we do know that that company sold her to the Alaska Packers' Association, also of San Francisco, in 1906. Under her new house flag, the stately *Star of Bengal* made regular voyages between San Francisco and Alaskan ports for the next two

The elegant *Star of Bengal* at anchor in Alaska with a steam sailor anchored in the background. ALASKA STATE LIBRARY HISTORICAL COLLECTIONS/ASL-P134A

years, taking general cargo north and almost always carrying fish, mostly cases of salmon, on the southbound run.

At the end of the 1908 season, she loaded the salmon at a Wrangell wharf and took on the scores of cannery workers. Her next stop was scheduled to be her home port of San Francisco. Two tugs took the *Star of Bengal* in tow to escort her through the difficult waters close to Wrangell, where wind and current could prove difficult for sailing ships. The tugs would leave her once she reached the open sea. The Alaskan weather, however, had different ideas.

Wrangell Island is located on the Alaska panhandle, on the Inside Passage between British Columbia and Alaska.

(It should not be confused with Wrangel Island, which is in the Arctic Ocean.) In shape, Wrangell Island resembles a tooth, with the town of Wrangell at the point of the root, in this case, on the northern extremity. It is about 15 miles wide from east to west and 30 miles long from north to south. To reach the open sea from the loading wharf at Wrangell, the ship and its attendant tugs had to set a course to take them west through Sumner Strait and make a sharp southwesterly turn at just beyond the halfway point. That would take the ship and tugs past the south side of Coronation Island.

Coronation Island is in an exposed position on the eastern edge of the North Pacific Ocean, due south of Cape Decision on Kuiu Island. On the route the tugs would have taken, the south coast of Coronation Island is approximately 80 miles from Wrangell. That distance, towing a heavy ship in a mounting storm, would have taken them from at least 8 to 12 hours. As the trio of ships came abeam of Coronation Island, working down into Iphigenia Bay with Warren Island off to port, the tugs were within a short distance of casting the windjammer free to set sail for the south. At that location, where the incoming ocean swells were huge, the capricious Alaskan weather interfered to change the plans.

The *Wrangell Sentinel* newspaper reported that Captain Farrar, of the Alaskan tug *Hattie Gage*, gave the following account of the loss of the *Star of Bengal* on the rocks of Coronation Island:

As we ran into the gale we could see we were making leeway and drifting toward Coronation Island. The other tug, the *Kayak*, was light and could do nothing. The *Hattie Gage* could not handle the ship alone. At 4 o'clock the *Star of Bengal* drifted into a narrow bight and we could see land on both sides abreast. We sounded and found eight fathoms. We could see the vessel dimly by the phosphorous rocks that were all around. We cut the towline and steamed out into open water. We could not see anything in the driving rain except one blue light burning on the ship. The storm increased and the tugs steamed to Shipley Bay [on Prince of Wales Island], twenty-six miles away.

The tugs had gone, and the *Star of Bengal* was helpless, stuck in a cove near Helm Point on the southernmost extremity of Coronation Island. She had both anchors out but was at the full mercy of the storm. While the crew fought to keep her off the land, the southwesterly storm pounded the ship, causing her to drag the anchors. Without that double security, she was driven ashore with no chance of getting off. Survivors later reported that one of the *Star of Bengal*'s boats did manage to get away with a few men on board and landed on Coronation Island safely. From the advantage of solid ground, they were able to help several more of their companions to reach land. They also pulled Captain Wagner off the wrecked ship. He was reported to have been unconscious for an hour and lost the power of speech for a while. Therefore, one assumes, he took no part in the rescue attempts.

In a desperate but commendably professional attempt at saving more lives, the onshore crew rigged a line from a tree to the ship, with the intention of using a breeches buoy to take off the rest of the crew and cannery workers. Unfortunately, the aggressive action of the wind and waves made the ship sway from side to side so violently that the line alternated between being too tight and in danger of breaking, and so loose that it dipped into the waves. Since the line could not be kept stable for more than a few seconds, it was too dangerous, if not impossible, to use.

One of the crew had somehow managed to get ashore with a box of matches in his clothing, which he had kept dry enough to use. He and others built a fire from driftwood; using kerosene from the wreck, they were able to stoke the bonfire enough to keep warm and avoid hypothermia.

When the news of the wreck on Coronation Island reached Wrangell, the cable ship *Burnside* got up steam and departed to look for survivors. Hours later, that ship's crew found the 27 exhausted men huddled around their seashore fire. The *Star of Bengal*'s books and papers were discovered scattered on the beach nearby, but the big windjammer was gone. She had been broken into three pieces by the storm and sent to the seabed. All that was left to see were the tips of three masts poking through the surface of the water. Of the dead, the only bodies recovered for burial were Benjamin Johnson, Siguard Nelson, Eric Pierson, William Perischke, Peter Peterson, John Peterson, Olaf Peterson, Einon

Swenson, Charles Buchanan, Carl Bore, Joseph Griffin, Andrew Hanson, Frank Healy, Norman Hawkins and G. Hendrickson. They were, presumably, all members of the crew, as the cannery workers, none of whom survived, were mostly Chinese and Japanese.

When the survivors reached Wrangell, courtesy of *Burnside*, Captain Wagner had harsh words for the skippers of the two tugs that had abandoned his ship. He accused them both of "rank cowardice." Whether or not he was justified in his criticism has never been determined. It is possible that they too were in danger from the incoming storm and left the windjammer to save their own much smaller vessels.

CHAPTER

9

Francis H. Leggett's Final Storm

SIXTY-FIVE PASSENGERS AND CREW died on the September 1914 afternoon that the 1,606-ton passenger and cargo ship *Francis H. Leggett* went to her grave. Most of them would have been terrified by the violence of the storm that pounded the small ship with such merciless power. Great grey-backed waves towered over *Francis H. Leggett* and broke into hundreds of tons of cascading water that filled every nook and cranny of the insignificant vessel's hull.

Francis H. Leggett was built of steel in Newport News, Virginia, and launched in April 1903. She was 241.5 feet long and had a beam of 41.2 feet. She wasn't pretty by any means, but she was a sturdy and functional craft. Designed to carry heavy loads of lumber as well as passengers, she was considered an inexpensive way to travel between Washington's Pacific-coast ports and San Francisco.

In mid-September 1914, the 11-year-old steam schooner loaded lumber and railroad ties at two sawmills in Hoquiam, Washington, in sheltered Gray's Harbor. After the cargo had been secured in holds and additional railroad ties strapped down on deck, the passengers went on board. Some had travelled down from Alaska, joined other passengers at Seattle and completed the journey to the ship by train. That contingent made up roughly half the passenger complement of 40 persons. The other half came from the various towns dotted around Gray's Harbor. They were all going to San Francisco.

The sea was calm when *Francis H. Leggett* steamed away from Hoquiam in the early evening of September 16. She was probably overloaded with cargo, and her passenger manifest was incomplete, but despite those illegalities, she had an extremely capable and experienced captain on the bridge. Captain Charles Maro and all on board were expecting a slow but uneventful short voyage to their California destination.

As the lumbering freighter crossed the Gray's Harbor bar and turned south, she ran into a gale from the southeast. Forcing her way into a headwind and rapidly building waves, the ship crawled down the coast through the night. From the mouth of Gray's Harbor to the gaping maw of the Columbia River is no more than 50 miles. *Francis H. Leggett* should have covered that distance in about five hours, but the increasingly violent storm held her back so that it took her a full 24 hours of hard going to gain the latitude of Astoria, on the south side of the Columbia River mouth. She radioed her position from there but made no comment about sea or weather conditions.

As the ship struggled south along the Oregon coast, making little headway, she rolled fore and aft and from side to side in a corkscrew motion. The constant twisting loosened her deck cargo, and it began to shift. This inevitably caused the ship to take on a list, dangerous at any time but potentially fatal in a storm. The seas had been breaking over the bow and sweeping across the decks for two days. Hammering at the ship and its cargo, the waves showed every indication of winning the unequal struggle.

Captain Maro asked the passengers to remain below for their own safety. His crew then risked their lives by cutting away the bindings holding the deck cargo of railroad ties and letting them wash overboard. The loss of weight must have stabilized the ship to an extent. It certainly should have helped to bring the ship up onto an even keel again, but it was too little too late.

A monster wave reared up over the bow and smashed down onto the decks, carrying a hatch cover away with it. That cargo hold, now open to the elements, quickly began to fill with water from the seas breaking over the ship. At that time, the engine room would have been safe from the incoming water due to the watertight bulkheads installed when the ship was built. As the open hold took on hundreds of gallons of water, the ship developed a starboard list. The radio operator sent out a distress signal, but no one answered. There was a ship just within the limited range of the endangered freighter, but she had a different agenda.

The First World War had started in late July 1914. German forces were invading neighbouring countries in Europe. While the US was neutral, Japan had joined European nations against the Teutonic threat. In September 1914, when *Francis H. Leggett* sent out her distress call, a Japanese naval cruiser was not far away. She was in the area hunting German warships known to be in the North Pacific. On hearing the mayday, *Idzumi*, the Japanese cruiser, sent a radio message to the Marconi station at Astoria, Oregon, to advise operators there of the freighter's plight, but the Japanese did not go to her assistance.

On board *Francis H. Leggett*, Captain Maro ordered passengers to put on life jackets and come up on deck. Another licensed skipper, Captain Jens Jensen, was on board as a passenger. While Captain Maro saw to his endangered ship, Captain Jensen helped by looking after the passengers.

Launching a lifeboat in mountainous seas has never been an easy task. Equally, persuading passengers to abandon a large ship in a storm and put their trust in a pathetically small boat requires an enormous leap of faith on their part. While Captain Maro wrestled with his ship on the bridge, Captain Jensen ordered the crew to lower a lifeboat and get the women into it first. James Farrell, a passenger, reported that Jensen threatened to shoot any man who failed to observe the priority order.

The first attempt at launching the lifeboat with only a handful of people in it was a failure. Heavy seas made the task impossible, so it was hauled up again before it could be swamped. A second attempt, with only two women volunteers and close to 30 men, was disastrous. The boat capsized as soon as it touched the agitated seas. None of those on board survived, although some were able to cling to floating railroad ties until their strength gave out.

Seeing their fellow passengers swept away to their deaths determined most of the remaining passengers to stick with the ship. In consequence, when a second lifeboat was launched with the same tragic result, only a few people were aboard. They too were lost. Less than half the original complement was left on the ship, and most of those had to suspect that they too were doomed.

James Farrell was helping to launch another lifeboat when the ship finally stopped fighting. He jumped overboard with a few others as *Francis H. Leggett* turned over and went down by the stern. Farrell said he went deep, probably drawn down by the suction as the ship foundered. He was made of stern material, however, and fought his way to the surface in time to see the ship's bow pointing at the sky before it slid out of sight. Farrell and others grabbed hold of floating railroad ties and draped themselves across them as best they could.

Being in the cold water and in mountainous waves was enough to kill most people, but to add to the survivors' terror, they had to contend with railroad ties that rocketed up from the depths of the sunken ship's cargo holds and decks. Many of those deadly wooden missiles exploded onto the surface, where they injured and perhaps killed some who might otherwise have survived. James Farrell estimated that perhaps as many as two dozen people had made it off the ship safely.

As the hours after the sinking dragged on, the floating passengers and crew succumbed one by one to hypothermia, injuries or despair. Soon only two men remained alive out of the 67 people who had sailed from the last Washington port.

Like James Farrell, passenger George Poelman wrapped his arms around floating debris and fought to stay alive. Neither knew of the other's proximity. They each rolled with the big swells and prayed for a passing ship to see them. They did not know it, but the distress call had been heard, and as a result, two ships were converging on the scene. The first to arrive was the tanker *Frank H. Buck*, followed soon after by the liner *Beaver*. *Buck*'s lookouts sighted drifting wreckage about 11 p.m. As she moved slowly through the debris looking for survivors, she came close to Poelman without anyone seeing him. But Poelman was not one to lie down and die. From some deep reserve inside him, he found the strength to bellow for help, and against all the odds, he was heard by someone on the nearby ship and rescued without a boat being launched.

About an hour after Poelman was lifted aboard *Frank H. Buck* and taken care of, a lookout with a searchlight saw another man clinging to a railroad tie. Picking the exhausted man up with a lifeboat was difficult in the heavy seas because the crew kept losing sight of him, but it was eventually accomplished. When they found Farrell, *Beaver* was the closest ship, so he was taken aboard her to be resuscitated.

The two ships searched the debris field for a long time. They recovered a few bodies but no more living persons. Some would have drifted out to sea; others went down trapped in the ship. The sea had claimed its price.

10

Princess Sophia's Clash with a Vanderbilt

THE LAST VOYAGE AT THE end of a long summer season is inevitably a bittersweet occasion. Ships' crews are looking forward to getting home and maybe taking some time off with their families. Passengers look back at the time spent ashore with a certain amount of nostalgia, while anticipating their arrival at a new or familiar destination. No crew member or passenger, however, expects that final run to end in a massive tragedy. But that is exactly what happened to the Canadian Pacific steamer *Princess Sophia* and all who sailed in her in late October 1918.

The sleek *Princess* stood at the dock in Skagway, Alaska, in sight of the railroad tracks on the east side of town. She was sheltered there from the wind that was beginning to whip the waters of the north end of Lynn Canal into armies of whitecaps. She had arrived at 1:00 p.m. that day at the completion of her scheduled four-day voyage from Vancouver's Burrard Inlet. En route, after her first stop— Alert Bay, on Vancouver Island's northern tip—she had made a slight detour to assist the SS *Alaska*, which had run aground near Swanson's Bay. As it happened, *Alaska* managed to free herself before help arrived and made for a nearby port with all passengers and crew safe.

Princess Sophia was no stranger to such mishaps. She had run aground twice herself—in April 1913 and in January 1914—with no casualties either time. Once her officers were assured there was nothing they could do to help *Alaska*, *Princess Sophia* continued, making calls at Prince Rupert and Juneau before completing the northbound voyage at Skagway.

With a strict timetable to keep, the passengers were disembarked and the cargo unloaded as fast as possible. Then, as the hours marched on, a new complement of passengers and baggage was taken aboard. Finally, at 10:10 p.m. on October 23, 1918, *Princess Sophia* departed Skagway for Vancouver. She was running just over three hours late, and a storm was threatening from the north. Captain Leonard Locke and pilot Jeremiah (Jerry) Shaw, who was also a licensed captain, were both on the bridge as Skagway fell behind. On board under their care were at least 353 people: 65 crew and 278 passengers, plus a handful of stowaways

Princess Sophia steaming north in 1912. She was considered to be the most luxurious ship on the Inside Passage run to Alaska.
WILLIAM KAYE LAMB, LIBRARY AND ARCHIVES CANADA C-002470

whose names were not on the passenger lists for obvious reasons. There were also 13 draft horses and 11 other horses, at least one dog and five tons of general freight.

Captain Locke was 66 years old and had been at sea for 50 years. He had been in command of *Princess Sophia* for the past two years. Captain Shaw, the pilot, was also acting as first officer for this voyage, as the regular first officer was on vacation. Apart from the vastly experienced officers and crew, the ship carried eight steel lifeboats and one of wood, plus six life rafts. In addition, she had 548 life preservers on board, more than enough for the passengers and crew members.

The brief run to join the Lynn Canal was smooth,

although snow was falling. As *Princess Sophia* turned left into Lynn Canal, she was hit hard by a driving snowstorm and winds howling directly down the canal from the north. Skippers who regularly sailed the Inside Passage to Alaska were used to bad weather. The 50-mile-per-hour winds and the thick snowstorm that night would have given no great cause for alarm to either Locke or Shaw. Caution, however, should have persuaded the captain to slow his ship by a few knots, even perhaps cut the speed in half until conditions improved. Despite the almost complete lack of visibility, Captain Locke aimed the ship down the centre of Lynn Canal and wound her up to her full speed of over 12 knots. He was more than three hours behind schedule, and he intended to make up that time, if possible.

Seventeen years before, the Canadian Pacific's *Islander* had hit an iceberg in Lynn Canal while running at full speed, with disastrous results. Nine years later, another of the company's ships, *Princess May*, ran up onto Sentinel Island Reef, southeast of Vanderbilt Reef, although that time no lives were lost and the ship was salvaged. And, of course, *Princess Sophia* had been called on to assist *Alaska* when she had run aground in Swanson's Bay. The Inside Passage, and Lynn Canal in particular, was no place for carelessness. But the memory of those other ships and their accidents failed to ring any warning bells for captains Locke and Shaw. They steamed blindly into the night, on course for the first stop: Juneau.

Lynn Canal is a long fjord, 10 miles across at its widest point. In some places, it is a couple of miles narrower. From Skagway, it stretches 90 miles until it divides in two to pass through the islands. There is nothing in the way for much of that distance, except Vanderbilt Reef, and that obstruction occupies a prime position in the south. About one acre in area, quite flat and only 15 feet above sea level at the lowest tide, it is often awash at high tide. It rises almost straight up from the seabed four miles from the west shore and two and a half miles from the east side of Lynn Canal. In 1918 it was marked only by an unlit buoy on the south side, visible in daylight and good weather to ships heading north but invisible to ships steaming south. At night, or in fog or whiteout conditions, the buoy was useless.

Most ships heading south from Skagway used Point Sherman as a land reference. When passing this obvious headland, they would alter course a little to either the east or west side of Lynn Canal in order to clear Vanderbilt Reef by a margin of a mile or more. Something went wrong on the October night that *Princess Sophia* raced south for the last time. Someone on the bridge, either Captain Locke or Captain Shaw, made an error in navigation and positioned the ship too close to the middle of Lynn Canal.

Less than four hours after leaving the dock at Skagway, *Princess Sophia* steamed into the almost invisible Vanderbilt Reef at close to full speed. Her momentum was such that she rode right up onto the reef, decelerating rapidly, and became suspended there, standing almost upright with her bow and stern both out of the water. Somehow, perhaps because many of the passengers were in bed, there were no serious injuries, although no word was said about the condition of the 24 horses and the dog.

The crew quickly ascertained that their ship was quite safe on the reef for the time being. Certainly, lodged in a groove as she was, there was no likelihood that she would suddenly slide off to either side and sink. The radio operator sent out a distress call, and Captain Locke had a message relayed to his superiors in Vancouver about the accident. Following standard procedures, Locke ordered the lifeboats swung out over the sides on their davits, but not lowered. Within very few hours of hearing the SOS, a small fleet of ships began leaving a variety of ports along the Inside Passage and made their best speed to aid *Princess Sophia*.

High tide was at 6:00 a.m., just under four hours after the ship hit the reef. With a sea running, the ship pounded on the reef, which would have unsettled the passengers and probably some of the crew. Captain Locke had hoped *Princess Sophia* would float free with the tide, but she stubbornly clung to the rock.

At daylight, some of the crew lowered a lifeboat. The handful of men inside inspected the condition of the ship's hull without the boat actually settling onto the water. When they were hauled back up, they reported the damage. At about that time, there were two relatively small ships standing by. Captain James Davis, master of the 65-foot-long mail and passenger boat *Estebeth*, studied the marooned ship and reported that "she had a big rent in the bow, fore and aft, and the water was pouring out of her in a big gush: running out say probably two or three hundred gallons a minute, something like that, [from a] probably four or six inch seam. Her propeller was just showing aft. [She was] resting very easy, probably wasn't two feet off her natural water line, that is fore and aft, and listing maybe five to ten percent to starboard."

Up to then, no attempt had been made to take any passengers off *Princess Sophia*. Captain Locke, it was said, felt it was too dangerous to launch lifeboats with the sea running high and the storm creating whitecaps. He believed his charges were safer on the steamer, despite her predicament.

Throughout that day the rescue boats waited. The passengers on *Princess Sophia* waited. Around 4 p.m., people were seen getting into one of her lifeboats, and it was lowered partway down, giving the impression to those on the waiting boats that the rescue was about to begin. It was, however, a false alarm. The lifeboat was raised again without touching the sea. Captain Locke had decided it was still too windy. His assessment of the situation was about to be severely tested by the elements. Instead of subsiding, the wind increased in intensity, and the storm built up again.

The attendant ships and boats, some of which had stood by all day, left to find shelter as dark fell, after receiving approval from Captain Locke. Only one vessel stayed close. The large fishing boat *King and Winge* remained in sight and on watch throughout the night, riding the storm and giving a modicum of confidence to the *Princess'* passengers. A couple of others were not far away, taking a rest from the wind and waves behind nearby islands and ready to return at a moment's notice if necessary.

The storm showed no signs of letting up. By 4 o'clock the next morning, as high tide approached, the waves were seen to be battering the stranded ship between her stern and midships. Other boats and ships began to return and circled the reef invitingly, but nothing could be done to take anyone off the ship. The wind was stronger; the waves were bigger. Launching a lifeboat into the whitewater breaking over the reef would be fatal. Everyone settled down to wait again.

In the late afternoon of October 25, about 40 hours after she skidded her bow up onto Vanderbilt Reef, *Princess Sophia* began to move again. As the storm increased in intensity from out of the north, the combined action of wind and waves picked up her stern. Once it was off the reef, the ship began a slow 180-degree turn, pivoting on a section of hull roughly amidships. Despite the covering noise of the storm, those on board would have heard the horrendous screaming noise of her ruptured hull scraping across the flat reef. No one knows how long it took the ship to complete the turn—probably not very long. The radio operator sent out an SOS at 4:50 p.m., just as the ship's stern began to swing

Princess Sophia stranded on Vanderbilt Reef in Alaska's Lynn Canal, October 24, 1918. WINTER-POND CO., JUNEAU, ALASKA. NOAA PHOTO LIBRARY

around, and a final message half an hour later. By that time, the ship's bow was pointing into the storm. She hesitated for a few seconds, and then, as if determined to find her natural element again, *Princess Sophia* began to slide backwards off the reef. The radio operator, desperate for help, said water was coming into the radio room. A few minutes later, the radio went silent.

No one knows for sure what the passengers and crew were doing as the *Princess* made her pirouette across the rock. Many of those who were not already wearing life jackets would have put them on. The bodies recovered later showed that. The lifeboats had been swung out on their davits, but left covered to keep the snow out. We know some of the lifeboats were launched, but their chances of remaining upright in the waves breaking over the reef were practically zero.

As the ship slid backwards off the reef, the rocks tore more gashes in her hull until most of her bottom was gone. All the passengers and crew who had not taken to the boats would have faced a dreadful decision: stay on board and pray the ship would not really sink, or risk jumping overboard into the blizzard and body-numbing freezing seas. Many of them did just that in a frantic but futile gamble to stay alive. They had waited so long for a rescue that never happened, and that desperate attempt at survival was their last chance.

There was more than just the storm to contend with, though. As the ship's hull was ripped apart, her bunkers ruptured and thousands of gallons of thick, sticky fuel oil spilled into the sea. The oil may have had a brief calming influence on the waves, but it spelled certain death for even those strong enough to swim.

Oil floats on water. As *Princess Sophia* went down, a vast amount of viscous oil spread quickly and thickly over the waters of Vanderbilt Reef. It blinded the swimmers, filled their lungs and choked them.

There were no survivors. The only creature to live through the wreck, the subsequent oil slick, the storm and the icy seas was a dog. The English setter, said to have been owned by one of the passengers, was found at Auk Bay,

12 miles from the wreck, two days after the ship sunk. The dog was covered in oil, terrified and starving, but it was alive. The 24 horses, like the human passengers and crew, drowned as the ship went down.

There are chilling echoes of SS *Islander*'s last hours in *Princess Sophia*'s story and perhaps a prophecy for the future. Both ships came to grief in Lynn Canal, part of the Inside Passage; both ships struck at about 2:00 a.m. Many years later, long after radar had been introduced and navigation lights had been installed along its length, and despite the most modern technology, another passenger ship would come to grief in the Inside Passage.

11

The Honda Point Fiasco

IT'S HARD TO BELIEVE THAT seven naval destroyers travelling together at 20 knots could all run aground at the same place within seconds of each other, but that is exactly what happened on the California coast on the night of September 8, 1923. A squadron of 14 US Navy destroyers, designated DESRON 11, were taking part in a simulated war exercise. Their charted course was south from San Francisco to San Diego via the Santa Barbara Channel. Led by USS *Delphy*, the flagship, under the command of Captain Edward H. Watson, the convoy steamed south at cruising speed in column formation. Just over 12 hours after leaving port, 23 men would die, and half the ships would be wrecked.

The 80-mile-long Santa Barbara Channel is often used

as a shortcut for ships travelling along the California coast between San Francisco and Los Angeles. It separates the California mainland from the eight pieces of offshore real estate that make up the northern Channel Islands. Like much of the California coast, the channel is no stranger to thick fogs. Its northern entrance is also notorious for high winds and heaving waves. The narrowest stretch is between Ventura, on the mainland, and Anacapa Island—no more than 20 nautical miles. The section east of Honda Point or, more correctly, Point Pedernales, is considered the most dangerous stretch.

The squadron of *Clemson*-class destroyers were navigating by dead reckoning, an imprecise procedure at the best of times. Radar had not yet been invented, and radio navigation aids, although available, were not considered completely trustworthy. *Delphy* did have a radio navigation receiver, but her commander and two navigators chose not to believe the bearings it gave them. Instead, they stuck to the traditional methods and paid a drastic price.

Many of the *Clemson*-class destroyers, particularly those of the Honda Point fiasco, were built by the Bethlehem Shipbuilding Corporation. They were 314 feet long and 31 feet in the beam. Displacing 1,215 tons, they could chase after an enemy vessel at just over 35 knots. They were fast, well equipped with weaponry, and they looked good. They all carried four funnels, which had earned them the popular nickname of "four-stackers."

Due to a navigational error, seven US Navy destroyers ran aground at Honda Point, California, on the night of September 8, 1923.
US NAVAL HISTORICAL CENTER #NH84821

On the night of September 8, the fast-moving convoy was north and east of where the navigators on *Delphy* believed the ships to be—a dangerous error. At 9:00 p.m., in darkness and thick fog, the convoy was ordered to a new course of 095 degrees. According to the navigators' dead reckoning, that should have taken them into the Santa Barbara Channel.

Five minutes after making the turn, *Delphy* came to an abrupt stop as she rammed broadside into jagged rocks at Honda Point and broke in half. Considering her speed, the sudden deceleration would have thrown all those on the bridge off balance, as well as anyone else aboard not braced. *Delphy* sounded her signal alarm immediately, but chaos ensued behind her. The next ship in line, a few hundred yards astern, was the USS *S.P. Lee*. Sharp eyes on her bridge saw *Delphy* stop suddenly and called for an immediate hard turn to port. It was a quick reaction, but it came too late. As the destroyer's wake began to curl behind her, *S.P. Lee* ran aground just north of *Delphy*. The officers aboard the USS *Young* seem to have completely missed what was happening ahead; she steamed right up onto the rocks just south of *Delphy*'s position and ripped her hull open. The sea poured in, and, way off balance, the *Young* rolled over onto her starboard side. Pandemonium broke out on board as sailors were thrown from one side of the ship to the other as she stopped abruptly and turned over.

The USS *Woodbury* made a quick turn to starboard to avoid the danger, but she hit a rocky islet and was holed. Trying to keep clear of the mayhem in front of her, the USS *Nicholas* turned to port and also found rocks, just beyond *S.P. Lee*. Then the USS *Fuller* steamed in, crumpled her bow on a rock and came to a stop near *Woodbury*. USS *Chauncey*'s captain, who had managed to keep his ship out of danger until then, took her in much too close to shore in an attempt to rescue the survivors of the *Young*, who could be seen holding onto the hull of their capsized ship for dear life. *Chauncey*'s rescue plan was valiant but came to grief when her hull was ripped open from bow to stern by *Young*'s propeller. She ended up on the rocks close by, but still upright.

Somehow, perhaps because of their position in the convoy or perhaps because they responded in time to the signal alarm from the flagship, the USS *Farragut* and the USS *Somers* managed to avoid serious damage. *Farragut* was next in line behind *Woodbury* and *Nicholas*. Her captain, Lt. Commander John F. McCain, saw the mayhem ahead and ordered the engines to full astern, too late to get completely out of danger. His ship ran aground, but he was able to get her off safely and without damage. *Somers* hit something solid and sustained light damage to her bow but stayed afloat. Quick action by the officers on the bridge of the USS *Percival* saved their destroyer from the rocks, although she only just missed them. The final four ships—*Kennedy, Paul Hamilton, Stoddert* and *Thompson*—scattered to left and right and headed back out to sea, where they could keep clear of the carnage and the coast.

For the crews on the seven wrecked destroyers, many so rudely awakened by the sudden collisions with land, a fight for survival began. It was dark and foggy, and they must have been disoriented. All around them were wrecked ships, deadly rocks and big waves breaking over everything.

When *Young* capsized, many of her engine- and fire-room crews were trapped below. The captain, Lt. Commander William Calhoun, ordered all physically able crew members to make their way up to the port side but to stay with the ship. Hauling a line behind him, Bosun's Mate Peterson dived into the surf and swam across to *Chauncey*, stuck on a rock about 75 yards away.

Despite their own perilous position, *Chauncey*'s crew continued their attempt to rescue their fellow sailors on the *Young*. They dragged the brave Peterson aboard and tied the line off. Soon a seven-man life raft was sent across from *Chauncey* to *Young*. It took 11 trips back and forth across angry seas before all *Young*'s 70 survivors reached *Chauncey*. Meanwhile, strong swimmers from *Chauncey* made it through the surf to the mainland and rigged lines from the two ships to the shore, enabling the survivors from *Young* and everyone on *Chauncey* to make their way to safety.

On *Woodbury*, water poured in through a gash in the forward hull. Down below, the engineers did their best to respond to a signal for full astern from the bridge. All their efforts came to naught as the inflow of sea water flooded the engines and boilers. On the foredeck, *Woodbury*'s crew ran four lines out from their ship and anchored them to the expansive rock beside them, hoping to get men across before the ship could sink. The incoming surf and breaking waves pounded *Woodbury* so much that although she had settled down by the stern, her bow rose and fell with the wave action. That fore and aft rolling motion threatened to rip the rigged lines from the rock. Somehow, no doubt due to the skill of the sailors who had anchored them, the lines were kept intact. When the captain, Commander Davis, gave the order to abandon ship, all on board were able to cross to the rock, "monkey fashion," by using the four fixed lines.

All the crew from the USS *Fuller* also made it to the comparative safety of the rock, where *Woodbury*'s crew waited for rescue. They were all eventually taken off, some by *Percival*, some by *Somers* and others by a fishing boat, *Bueno Amor de Roma*. *Fuller* later broke in two and sunk.

Lt. Commander Herbert Roesch, the captain of *Nicholas*, fought to save his ship as she was battered against the rocks by breaking waves. The sea and its currents had different plans. They pushed the ship, stern first, onto a rock until her stern was out of the water. She stopped there, listing 25 degrees to starboard. By morning, the captain accepted that there was nothing more he could do to save his destroyer. With a heavy heart, he gave the order to abandon ship. It is to his credit that everyone on board reached the nearby shore safely. The crew of *S.P. Lee* also gave up the fight to save their ship that morning. Closer in to land than *Nicholas*, they too were all saved.

Twenty men died on *Young*, and three more died on *Delphy*. All were enlisted men. Eleven of the twenty who died on *Young* were firemen, working deep inside the ship; another was an engineman. Two of the three deaths on *Delphy* were also firemen. Hundreds of others were injured on the seven destroyers, fifteen of them on *Delphy*.

Inevitably, the blame for the disaster was set squarely on the commodore's shoulders, but Captain Watson was not the only one found guilty. The US Navy court of inquiry also laid blame on the navigators and captains of each of the seven wrecked ships. Considering that 23 men were lost, in addition to seven valuable warships, the sentences handed down were extremely light. The heaviest sentences simply took away much of the seniority of the officers involved. Although none of them would rise to higher command, no one went to jail.

12

The End of
Ohioan's Career

THE CALIFORNIAN COAST AND SEA fog: put them together and they spell disaster for the unwary who sail near the rugged shores, as so many ships' crews have learned to their ultimate cost. On the night of October 8, 1936, the SS *Ohioan* was steaming along the coast in dense fog when she ran aground near Seal Rock, on the south shore of the Golden Gate. Her impact was so severe that it sent a large shower of sparks into the night, like a private fireworks display. A cargo ship, she was carrying a volatile cargo of explosives and oil.

The *Ohioan* was built by the Maryland Steel Company and launched in June 1914 for the American-Hawaiian Steamship Company. She was 6,649 GRT (gross registered tons) and measured 407 feet 7 inches from bow to stern, with a beam of 53 feet 8 inches. She was oil-fired, with a single propeller that gave her a cruising speed of about 12 knots. Her personnel consisted of 18 officers and 40 deck and engine-room crew.

Ohioan's first voyage was from east-coast ports of the United States, around the southern tip of South America via the Straits of Magellan, to west-coast ports and Hawaii. She carried general cargo from the east to the west and sugar and pineapples in the reverse direction. When the Panama Canal opened on August 15, 1914, the length of her voyages was drastically reduced, and her cargoes reached their owners in half the time.

The *Ohioan*'s First World War history is vague. She might have been chartered for trans-Atlantic use, or she could have worked the South America run. What is known is that she was absorbed into the US Navy and commissioned as USS *Ohioan* (ID-3280) on August 7, 1918. The navy's latest ship crossed the North Atlantic to St. Nazaire, on France's Bay of Biscay coast, arriving on August 29 with a full load of unspecified cargo.

Once unloaded, she was fitted with horse stalls for the return ocean crossing. One month after her arrival in France, she sailed home from Brest with 60 American army officers and men, plus horses and general cargo. On November 1, she again headed east, this time to La Pallice, France, also on the Bay of Biscay, and was back in the US by early December. The war was over by then, and a lot of American soldiers needed transport home. Accordingly, USS *Ohioan* was converted from a cargo-and-animal transport to a troopship.

The installation of bunks, cooking facilities, toilets and other amenities took a couple of months, maybe more. Once she was ready, she steamed for Europe at her best speed. There, 1,627 soldiers waited for her to take them to New York. In April 1919, she carried another 1,596 soldiers home. Also on that voyage, she catered to 1,000 homing pigeons and an additional 100 captured German pigeons. Over the next few months, *Ohioan* shuttled back and forth across the Atlantic to bring the troops back home. Six times she made the crossing in each direction, carrying an impressive total of 8,383 soldiers home from war. Among them was the hero of the Meuse-Argonne Offensive, Sergeant Alvin York. He had led his men in an attack on a German machine-gun emplacement, overpowered it and captured 132 enemy officers and men. When he arrived in New York, he proudly wore his medals—the US Medal of Honor and the French Croix de Guerre with Palm—on his jacket.

The USS *Ohioan* was decommissioned on October 6, 1919, and returned to her original owners. Before she could resume cargo service, all the trappings of a troopship had to be removed: hundreds of narrow bunks, plus the additional cooking and toilet facilities installed nearly a year before.

For the next 17 years, the now-civilian SS *Ohioan* transported a variety of cargoes on routine voyages between

USS *Ohioan* in port as a troopship during the First World War. She was built as a freighter for the American-Hawaiian Steamship Company. US NAVAL HISTORICAL CENTER #NH103055

ports on the east and west coasts, via the Panama Canal. On the last of those cruises, after picking up a pilot to take her into San Francisco, she ran into trouble because of thick fog, as so many other ships had done.

The morning after she struck Seal Rock, when the fog cleared, she was seen to be on the rocks only 300 feet from shore and a cliff 250 feet high. At that point, the crew were in no danger. They hoped to be able to float her off at the next high tide. Only the pilot wanted to get to land. The US Coast Guard took care of that; they fired three lines over to the ship from the cliff and rigged a breeches buoy to take him off.

Being in an exposed position and with the fog dispersed, *Ohioan* was visible to anyone who cared to look. The city of San Francisco was close by, and before long, the curious began to collect along the cliffs to stare at the stranded ship. The few onlookers became many, and the many became thousands. The crowd grew so big that police had to be called out to keep control. Newsboys were said to be selling their papers, which reported the news of the accident, in full view of the ship. With so many people converging on one place, it was inevitable that problems would occur. Two women broke their ankles, and one man died from a heart attack.

The next tide was not high enough to refloat *Ohioan*. As it reached its maximum height, the ship remained on the rocks. The next day the weather turned, and big waves rolled in, driving the freighter farther up onto the rocks and pounding her in a relentless procession of breakers. The crowds came back again. They stood and watched as a couple of coast guard boats took 31 men off the ship. They watched, too, as a pair of heavy-duty electric pumps were sent out to the ship by breeches buoy in an effort to pump her out.

The salvage efforts proved fruitless. The ship would not move, and there was no efficient way to offload the dangerous cargo. Still the crowds watched. On October 13, five days after the ship ran aground, a 75-year-old woman was almost killed when she fell over the cliff. Six more days went by with *Ohioan* no closer to being salvaged. The curious watched from the cliff and from the beach. Even Angelo Rossi, the mayor of San Francisco, decided to get into the act. He was transferred to *Ohioan* by breeches buoy and spent close to an hour wandering all over the ship.

At the end of October, the American-Hawaiian Steamship Company put out a call for bids to purchase the wreck and its cargo. The highest bidder was E.J. Mitchell, who bought ownership for a mere $2,800. Five months went by, and the wreck stayed where it was. Some of the cargo apparently stayed on board, although it seems that the oil must have been taken off. *Ohioan* had been battered quite badly by the winter waves, but she was still upright. Also, a watchman was aboard, mostly to deter potential scavengers from looting the ship. The watchman almost blew her up singlehandedly when he accidentally set her on fire. Fortunately, the flames extinguished themselves before they could burn their way through to the explosives in one of the holds.

The following December, a storm continued the work of previous bad weather. As a result of the assault by wind and waves, *Ohioan* broke in two and was finished. By the end of the 1930s, the only signs that a ship had once stranded on the rocks just offshore were a few rusting steel beams.

CHAPTER

13

Benevolence toward *Mary Luckenbach*

FOG AND NARROW BODIES OF sea water tend to invite shipping disasters. The Golden Gate, entrance to San Francisco and its beautiful bays, where fog is a part of daily life, has seen more than its share of catastrophes. Long before the magnificent suspension bridge was completed in 1937, the narrow strait cutting through the headlands required strong navigational skills. The Golden Gate strait is roughly three miles long and one mile wide. The currents coursing through the narrow gap run from 4.5 to 7.5 knots. When the bridge was completed, it was painted in a bright colour known as international orange in order to make it more visible, especially in fog. As such, it became a welcome visual aid to navigation for ships entering or leaving San Francisco's harbour.

At 8:00 a.m. on August 25, 1950, the hospital ship USS *Benevolence* left the Mare Island Naval Shipyard opposite the city of Vallejo, California, to spend a day on sea trials. She cruised down San Pablo Bay toward the city of San Francisco. After passing Sausalito on her starboard side, she made a right turn to take her under the Golden Gate Bridge to the Pacific Ocean. With just over 500 crew and other military and civilian personnel on board, *Benevolence* spent the next few hours at sea while a team of naval and Military Sea Transportation Service (MSTS) officers assessed her for duty with the service. The MSTS had been formed less than a year before to cater to all branches of the US military.

Thick fog blanketed the Golden Gate Bridge and the coast as the 15,450-ton *Benevolence* headed back toward the bay in the afternoon. Lightly laden, the 520-foot-long hospital ship sat high out of the water. Her clean white hull with a huge red cross on each side made her stand out, even in the fog. She was an impressive sight.

Meanwhile, another ship was preparing for sea. The SS *Mary Luckenbach* was an American freighter of 8,162 gross tons. She was 441 feet long and 63 feet across her beam and had been built in Wilmington, North Carolina, in 1944. On August 25, 1950, *Mary Luckenbach* slipped her moorings and steamed away from San Francisco. She was bound for Philadelphia by way of the Panama Canal. Her cargo for that voyage was 10,000 tons of general freight. Captain Leonard C. Smith was on the bridge as the ship took the centre channel through the Golden Gate. The other officers and crew, numbering 44 people, were either at their duties or off watch. The ship's radar was not functioning properly; that fault was said to be due to a lack of special training by its operators. In fact, the radar had not been in use since the ship passed Alcatraz Island soon after departure.

At 4:35 p.m., *Mary Luckenbach* passed under the Golden Gate Bridge. At that time the ship was travelling at an estimated 12 knots in thick fog, with visibility down to between 300 and 400 yards. A tidal current of 1.5 knots was running with the ship, increasing her actual speed to 13.5 knots. At that rate, a ship can cover 400 yards in just about one minute. Stopping takes much longer. *Mary Luckenbach*'s foghorn, or steam whistle, was sounded at regular intervals as required by maritime law, but Captain Smith did not reduce speed.

At the same time, *Benevolence* was approaching the Golden Gate from the opposite direction, steaming at an estimated 15 knots. Although her radar had a range of at least 15,000 yards, the operator failed to see the obvious blip denoting another ship dead ahead. The combined speed of the two ships, on a collision course, was over 28 knots. *Benevolence* too was sounding her foghorn as required.

At 4:51 p.m., those on board *Mary Luckenbach* heard one blast from a foghorn dead ahead. Captain Smith immediately ordered the engines stopped, then to full astern. One minute later, the bow wave of an approaching ship was seen

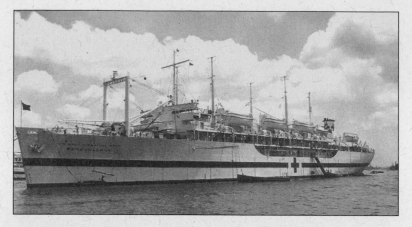

The US Navy hospital ship *Benevolence* at Pearl Harbor, Hawaii, in July 1945. Five years later, just outside San Francisco, she was in a fatal collision with the freighter *Mary Luckenbach*. US NAVAL ARCHIVES G-35488

about 400 yards away. Captain Smith ordered the helm to hard right, while signalling danger with four blasts of the foghorn.

A civilian pilot, Captain Lyle Havens, was conning *Benevolence*, and her senior officers were also on the bridge, as was her commander, Captain Bacon. Three enlisted men stood lookout watch in the bow. At 4:50, the pilot heard a fog signal dead ahead. He rang down to the engine room for "all stop." Even without the engines driving her, the ship was still racing forward at close to 15 knots. Two minutes passed, then another foghorn blast was heard, much nearer this time. With that, *Mary Luckenbach*'s creamy white bow wave showed through the fog, coming straight at *Benevolence*.

Captain Havens ordered right full rudder and called for two-thirds speed ahead. *Benevolence*'s single propeller thrashed the water at her stern to speed her out of the way of the rapidly approaching danger. Despite the actions of officers on both ships to avoid disaster, *Mary Luckenbach* crashed into *Benevolence* at 4:55 p.m. The two ships met "with terrific impact," port side to port side, at an angle estimated to be between 10 and 20 degrees.

Both ships heeled over to starboard, and the freighter struck the hospital ship again, though with less force, directly under the bridge deck. *Mary Luckenbach*'s captain called for hard left rudder and sounded a general alarm as his ship passed the stern of *Benevolence*. Eight minutes after the collision, the freighter dropped anchor in the fog and out of sight of the other ship. Damage control showed that "the port anchor had carried away, one set of bitts, port side carried away, port side set in about five feet from stem to hawse pipe." In addition, the port side of the bridge structure had been damaged, and the forepeak was flooded. She was, however, in no danger of sinking, but she did send out a distress signal.

While the crew of *Mary Luckenbach* assessed the damage to their ship, *Benevolence* was in trouble. The collision had caused a considerable gash in her port side. The enormous hole, varying from 3 to 5 feet above the waterline and extending upwards between 5 and 10 feet, was 50 feet long. As a consequence, the ship's compartments quickly filled with water. Although the engines had been stopped and the impact had taken the way off her, she was listing to port. The ship was obviously seriously damaged, but the captain did not order the lifeboats lowered. He instructed the radio-room personnel to send out an SOS, but that proved impossible, as the antenna had been disconnected.

As *Benevolence*'s list to port became more pronounced, it would have been impossible to launch lifeboats from either side. The official report into the accident stated that the captain did not give the order to abandon ship because he did not believe the ship would sink. Out of a total of 16 lifeboats aboard the hospital ship, only one, a whaleboat, was launched. Sixteen life rafts were on board, and some did get released, though no number was given. Between them, the lifeboats and the life rafts could carry in excess of 1,800 people, more than enough for the numbers aboard the ship that day.

Despite what her captain thought, *Benevolence* was sinking. The port list increased to 45 degrees, and she was down by the bow. Five minutes after the collision, her foredeck was at sea level. By this time, her complement of 500-plus sailors and civilians were jumping overboard to save themselves.

The whaleboat from *Benevolence* picked up 35 survivors and, taking two life rafts in tow carrying another 50 survivors, made its way to where *Mary Luckenbach* stood at anchor. The fog swirled around them as other boats came on the scene in response to the distress call. They included fishing boats, yachts, navy and army tugs and coast guard vessels. There were so many people in the water crying for help that the rescue boats were kept busy for hours. Captain Bacon was among the survivors. He floated in a lifebelt for at least two hours before being picked up. Between them, the fleet of small boats rescued hundreds of people, but despite their best efforts, 23 perished that day, all from the hospital ship. One of those who died was the pilot, Captain Lyle Havens.

Benevolence took just 25 minutes from the time of the collision until she rolled over on her side and disappeared from sight in 75 feet of water. *Mary Luckenbach* hauled her anchor shortly before midnight and steamed back to San Francisco, arriving at 2:30 a.m. On board were four of the survivors from *Benevolence*.

Mindful of the fact that the Korean War had started only a few weeks before, one official commented with a sense of relief that *Benevolence* could have been carrying 1,500 or more patients on board, instead of the relatively small number of 500 personnel. In the official inquiry, the captains of both ships were found to be guilty of running their ships at excessive speeds in thick fog.

CHAPTER

14

The Night a *Queen* Died

THE STORIES OF THE *PRINCESS SOPHIA* disaster of 1918 and the earlier *Islander* tragedy perhaps should be required reading for all mariners who conduct passengers through the Inside Passage. It might seem rather incredible in this constantly evolving age of technology, but 88 years after *Princess Sophia* took over 350 souls to their destiny, another ship, also travelling at night, came to grief in the confined but sensationally beautiful waterway.

At one minute to midnight, March 21, 2006, an elegant white ship steamed at full speed down Wright Sound, part of the Inside Passage, en route from Prince Rupert, on the mainland of British Columbia, to Port Hardy on the northern tip of Vancouver Island. The night was dark, except for the blaze of lights from the ship. It was raining lightly and quite windy. The weather, however, had no effect on the ship's progress. Of the 101 people aboard, 3 of the crew were on the bridge; others were working at their assigned tasks within the ship or on deck. Engineers were monitoring the engines. Catering staff were cooking meals; one was cleaning the galley. Some of the passengers were sleeping, and some were talking in the lounges. It was a normal night on a voyage that had taken place hundreds of times in each direction—normal except for one as yet unknown fact: in exactly 26 minutes the passenger and car ferry *Queen of the North* would tear her bottom out on a rocky island.

Queen of the North was built in Bremerhaven, Germany, in 1969 and launched as *Stena Danica* in the service of a Swedish company. She was stylish, looking like a mini cruise liner. In 1974 she was sold to BC Ferries and made the long voyage across the Atlantic and through the Panama Canal to the west coast. There, she entered service as the MV *Queen of Surrey*, working the route from Horseshoe Bay, on the mainland, to Departure Bay, Nanaimo, on Vancouver Island. She only served the route for a couple of years, then was given a four-year layoff. In 1980 she was brought out of the Delta yard on the Fraser River and reassigned to the Inside Passage: specifically, the Port Hardy to Prince Rupert route. She was also renamed *Queen of the North*.

Early in March 2006, she rested at a berth at the BC Ferries terminal in Tsawwassen after her annual refit.

She was sparkling clean and elegant to see. She was preparing to sail for Port Hardy, on the northern tip of Vancouver Island, to begin service on the Inside Passage run to Prince Rupert. When she steamed away on March 3, heading north up the Strait of Georgia, none who saw her leave could have imagined that in less than three weeks she would be lost.

The *Queen of the North* could carry 115 cars and up to 650 passengers, all looked after by a crew of 65. In the late spring and summer, she was usually full, but fortunately it was early in the season and the ship was lightly loaded. Official reports later stated that only 101 people were on board. Of those, 42 were crew and 59 were passengers. Among the passengers were 5 BC Ferries employees, although they were not part of the ship's crew. Apart from the paying passengers in the upper lounges, there were only 16 vehicles on the car deck to offset the costs of the voyage.

At 10:00 p.m., the *Queen of the North* sounded her steam whistle and pulled away from the dock at Prince Rupert. On the bridge, Captain Colin Henthorne supervised the departure. With him were the second officer, the fourth officer and a quartermaster. As is customary, the quartermaster— a deckhand—was steering the ship. On the *Queen of the North*, quartermasters steered the ship for one hour at a time before being relieved. Quartermaster no. 7 was on duty at departure and was visibly nervous in the restricted waterways of the harbour.

Once away from the dock, but still within the harbour

limits, Captain Henthorne handed over the navigational watch to the second officer and retired to his cabin to sleep for a while. At 10 minutes before 11 p.m., another deckhand arrived on the bridge to take over the helm as quartermaster. He waited until his eyes adjusted to the dark night before verifying the ship's position, course, speed and the weather. Then, with permission from the second officer, he took the helm.

All on the bridge were alert as the *Queen of the North* approached Ormiston Point on Pitt Island. The Grenville Channel, through which the ship had to pass, is only 500 yards wide at that point. Narrow enough in daytime, at night it requires the utmost navigational care. Once past the potential danger and entering a wider part of the channel, the second officer relieved the quartermaster at the helm and ordered the autopilot engaged. The quartermaster remained on the bridge as a lookout. At this time, there was nothing to suggest that the voyage would be any different from all the others. That would change suddenly in a little over an hour.

Other vessels were in the area that night. The fishing vessel *Lone Star*, a 37-foot shrimper, was running south on almost the same course as *Queen of the North*. Both vessels were experiencing a 20-knot wind hitting their starboard bows. Another fishing boat, the 40-foot shrimper *Sandra M*, had been passed by the much faster *Queen* and so had fallen behind. The Canadian Coast Guard ship *Sir Wilfrid Laurier* was at anchor in Bernard Harbour. There was also a tug not far away: *Castle Lake* was moving north very slowly, towing a log boom to Prince Rupert.

The quartermasters changed again at 10 minutes before midnight. With the ship on autopilot, quartermaster no. 7 took over lookout duties. The autopilot can be disengaged with a simple switch, which would have enabled the quartermaster to take over the helm at a moment's notice. The fourth officer was then in charge on the bridge, the second having gone for his break.

It was just after midnight. Music was playing on the bridge, and the navigational watch reported in by radio to Prince Rupert Traffic as they passed Sainty Point. The night was very dark, and no lights were visible. By this time, *Lone Star* had changed her course to round Waterman Point and run between Promise Island and the mainland to gain shelter from high crosswinds.

On the bridge, there was a less-than-desirable situation. Reports said that the female quartermaster and one of the male officers on the bridge that night had only recently ended a personal relationship with each other, but they still had to work together and at that moment bore the responsibility for guiding the big ship safely and professionally. Whether or not that reported relationship had any bearing on subsequent events is unknown.

The quartermaster followed the fourth officer's instructions; later the bridge crew claimed that that included

The MV *Queen of the North* served British Columbian ports between Prince Rupert and Port Hardy until she hit a rocky island and sank in 2006. BC FERRIES

making one or two slight course corrections, although the ship's electronic recorder showed no such changes. No one seemed to be aware of it, but the ship was approximately one nautical mile off its intended track. The *Queen of the North* was hustling south at 17.5 knots when the fourth officer ordered a drastic course change in a loud voice. The startled quartermaster questioned the order before complying. Looking out the windows, she saw the dark shadows of trees where no trees should be. At 22 minutes past midnight, the passenger and car ferry *Queen of the North* hit the rocky shore of Gil Island. She struck bow first and then hit again toward the stern on the starboard side. The engines were still running until the spinning starboard propeller hit, stalling them. The propeller was broken, and the ship ground to a halt. Subsequent study of the rocks in the vicinity showed the obvious stain of bottom paint and abrasion where the ship and rocks had met so violently.

Captain Henthorne was awakened by screaming and shouting and the dreadful sound of his ship grinding on granite. He and other off-duty officers reached the bridge quickly. The captain discovered the engine controls set at full astern, but the main engines were silent. The engine room was flooding, and the senior engineer ordered his crew to evacuate. As they left, they closed watertight doors behind them.

Alarms sounded throughout the ship, in the crew's quarters and in the passenger areas. The PA system ordered passengers to muster on the outer deck. Fortunately, unlike the grounding of the *Princess Sophia*, the night was relatively calm, apart from the crosswind. Getting the lifeboats off would not be a problem. While the passengers put on life jackets and made their way to the outside deck, the crew checked the lounges and pounded loudly on cabin doors to make sure no one was left behind. Red rocket flares lit up the sky as *Queen of the North* announced her plight. The radio sent out the message: *Queen of the North* is on the rocks of Gil Island. She was listing to starboard but afloat. She was also drifting slowly north from Gil Island in response to the wind and current.

As rescue boats raced to the scene, including a flotilla of small boats from Hartley Bay, a community about seven miles to the north, the passengers and crew abandoned ship. It seemed that everyone got away safely—or so the officers believed after doing a head count. Two people, however, had been left behind.

Watched by passengers and crew from the lifeboats, *Queen of the North* slowly settled lower in the water. The sea was calm, but a light rain fell, restricting visibility a little. At 1:40 a.m. on March 22, 2006, the stately car and passenger ferry began to go down stern first. People on a rescue boat watched as her bow rose in the air, noticing the amount of damage to the bow bulb and the forward hull. The official inquiry stated, "The bow angled steeply upward, exposing approximately the forward third of the ship, and then slipped beneath the surface, accelerating in the descent. As the ship sank, trapped air caused numerous windows on the passenger decks to explode outward, and a cloud of dust was formed at the scene."

Five minutes after the ship went to the bottom, *Lone Star* arrived on the scene. She was followed 11 minutes later by a fast rescue boat from *Sir Wilfrid Laurier*, running ahead of the mother ship. The coast guard vessel arrived at 2:10 a.m. and took command of the rescue efforts.

Sixty-three of the survivors were taken to Hartley Bay in small boats. Thirty-six others were taken aboard *Sir Wilfrid Laurier*. Inexplicably, considering the orderly manner in which the crew got themselves and the passengers off the ship, no one remembered to retrieve the ship's logbook.

Four days after the sinking, a manned submersible located the wreck. She sits upright on the seabed in quiet repose. Her stern is a little lower than the bow, a result of the plunge backwards to the bottom, but she is intact. Due to the soft nature of the seabed in the area, the ship has embedded herself in the silt up to her rubbing strakes level with the car deck. Her bottom, therefore, is concealed, making examination of the lower part of her hull impossible. The water where she rests is deep: 420 metres down, or roughly 1,410 feet below the surface.

Ninety-nine people survived what could have been a terrible tragedy. Sadly, the two people who somehow remained on board are believed to have gone down with the ship. The court cases to apportion blame and bring those responsible to trial continue as this book goes to press.

Epilogue

THE LONG COASTLINE BETWEEN CALIFORNIA and Alaska is safer now than it has ever been. Lighthouses and lightships mark formerly unseen hazards. Autopilots have been installed on most ships, and radar is now standard equipment, even on quite small boats. Day and night, in fair weather and foul, its sharp eyes allow navigators to see where other ships are positioned in relation to theirs and where land formations intrude on the sea. Global positioning systems, the ubiquitous GPS, not only tell ships and aircraft their location to within a few yards, but now decorate even the dashboards of cars. The installation of those and other modern navigational devices, however, does not protect drivers from error. The same is true of boats and ships on the sea. As seen in the sad story of the sinking of the Canadian car and passenger ferry *Queen of the North* in March 2006, human error can never be discounted. Of all the wrecks that now are in the process of becoming artificial reefs and havens for undersea life, far too many met their ultimate fate because of a moment's carelessness on the part of a captain, a navigator, an officer of the watch or another distracted crew member. Human error is still one of the greatest dangers at sea.

Selected Bibliography

"The Alaskan Founders." *The New York Times*. May 17, 1889.

"Another Survivor Reports." *The New York Times*. February 25, 1901.

BC Ferries. "Divisional Inquiry—*Queen of the North,* Grounding and Sinking. DI #815-06-01."

Belyk, Robert C. *Great Shipwrecks of the Pacific Coast*. New York: Wiley, 2001.

Coates, Ken, and Bill Morrison. *The Sinking of the Princess Sophia*. Anchorage: University of Alaska Press, 1991.

"Destroyers." *Dictionary of American Naval Fighting Ships Online*. www.hazegray.org/danfs/destroy.

"The Golden Gate Wreck." *The New York Times*. February 24, 1901.

Hice, Charles. *The Last Hours of Seven Four Stackers*. Miamisburg, OH: The Ohioan Company, 1967.

Library and Archives Canada. "Investigating the Islander." Shipwreck investigations. www.collectionscanada.gc.ca/sos/shipwrecks/002031-5200-e.html. Accessed March 7, 2010.

Lockwood, Charles A., and Hans Christian Adamson. *Tragedy at Honda*. Philadelphia: Chilton Company, 1960.

Newell, Gordon, ed. *The H.W. McCurdy Marine History of the Pacific Northwest*. Seattle: Superior Publishing, 1966.

Overshiner, Elwyn E. *Course 095 to Eternity*. Arroyo Grande, CA: Helm Publishing, 1990.

"Ship sinks off Alaska, dead number 110." *Cranbury Press*. October 2, 1908.

"Steamer Reported Lost." *The New York Times*. September 11, 1897.

Trudeau, Noah Andre. "A Naval Tragedy's Chain of Errors." *Naval History Magazine* 24, no. 1 (February 10, 2010). www.usni.org/magazines/navalhistory/2010-02/naval-tragedys-chain-errors.

"Tugs Left Sinking Ship." *The New York Times*. September 24, 1908.

United States Coast Guard internal communication. *Marine Board of Investigation; collision SS MARY LUCKENBACH and MSTS Ship BENEVOLENCE, entrance San Francisco Bay, 25 August, 1950, with loss of life.* Washington, DC, 1951.

Index

Acknowledgements

This book is about shipwrecks, so my initial accolades must go to my fellow explorers James Delgado and John Pollack. In separate ways, Jim and John both added fuel to my already considerable interest in ships and disasters—at sea and on large lakes and big rivers. Almost every conversation we have shared has at some point turned toward the search for sunken ships. Compared to professional underwater archaeologists such as Jim Delgado and John Pollack, I am an amateur, but I am enthusiastic and soak up information like a sponge. Whether they were aware of it or not, Jim and John taught me so much. Thanks, guys. I have enjoyed your company, and I cherish the lessons I have learned from you both.

Most of the factual information contained in this book about the various shipwrecks is a matter of record. To build my stories, I spent hours reading materials in books, magazines, official accident reports and more than a few websites. My thanks go to the authors of each of those documents for showing me the way forward. I am indebted to you all.

A Long, Dangerous Coastline and its predecessor, *The Graveyard of the Pacific*, would not have been written without the persuasion and support of Rodger Touchie, the publisher of Heritage House, and Vivian Sinclair, the managing editor. I am indebted to you both for your continued involvement in my literary career. A big thank you also goes to my editor, Lesley Reynolds, for making the editing process on this and *The Graveyard of the Pacific* such a comfortable experience.

About the Author

Anthony Dalton is the author of nine non-fiction books, many of which are about the sea or ships and boats. These include *The Graveyard of the Pacific, Polar Bears, Baychimo: Arctic Ghost Ship* and *Alone Against the Arctic*, all published by Heritage House. Anthony is the national president of the Canadian Authors Association and is currently working on a book about about shipwrecks of the Hudson's Bay Company for Heritage House's *Amazing Stories* series. He divides his time between homes on the mainland and in the Gulf Islands of British Columbia.